JOY SNELL

THE
MINISTRY OF ANGELS
Here and Beyond

The Citadel Press
New York

First American edition, April, 1959. Library of Congress Catalog Card
Number 59-8907. Manufactured in the United States of America. Pub-
lished by The Citadel Press, 222 Fourth Avenue, New York 3, N. Y.

Dedicated to those
Who mourn their dead

This book sets forth what one woman has learned of the Ministry of Angels on earth, and of life in other spheres of existence beyond this world.

It has been written because angels have told her that rare psychic powers have been bestowed on her, and she has been permitted to see what is hidden from the vast majority of mankind until after death, that she might tell others something of what has been revealed to her.

It is now sent forth in the earnest hope that it may be the means of bringing comfort to some of the millions in many lands who mourn their dead.

THE MINISTRY OF ANGELS
Here and Beyond

ONE

$\mathcal{T}$*he first* of my many strange experiences, from which I long ago learned that at times I see things which to most people are invisible, and hear sounds which to them are inaudible, occurred when I was twelve years old. With a brother two years older than myself, I was then living with an aunt in the north of Ireland. My father, a captain in the British army, was stationed in India.

I awoke one night to find the room filled with light, as though flooded with sunlight, and pervaded by a delicious odor such as emanates from the most exquisitely fragrant flowers, but the fragrance was imbued with an exhilarating quality that is not possessed by any perfume with which I am acquainted.

I heard a rushing sound, like that which might be made by the beating of many wings, and suddenly there appeared, standing in the middle of the room, two forms. One was that of a man, the other that of a woman. They were clad in shining white robes. Around the head of each was a bright halo. The man stretched forth his hand and said:

"Be not dismayed; blessed shalt thou be."

Then the woman spoke and said:

"Behold the Savior! And I am His mother."

The face of the man was bearded and his hair was long, falling below the shoulders; both beard and hair were of a reddish hue. The features closely resembled those of the traditional portraits of the Savior. But in most of them the predominant expression is one of sadness, while the face which I beheld expressed joy far beyond that which I have ever seen depicted on any human face. And yet there was that about it which proclaimed infinite compassion.

The face of the woman was of an oval type, very beautiful and aglow with love and tenderness. It was that which impressed me more than its beauty.

The figures slowly faded from my sight and the room was again dark. I was possessed by the feeling that the vision foreboded my own speedy death. For an hour or more I paced the floor with a beating heart, striving vainly to resign myself to that which I believed was inevitable. Then I became more composed and returned to my bed, but not to sleep, for I feared that I should not live to see the light of another day.

For three or four days this fear of impending death haunted me. A very dear friend, a sweet old Scotch lady whom everybody loved and in whom everybody confided, noticed that I was looking troubled and asked me what ailed me. I told her of the vision I had seen and that I was afraid it portended my death.

"Have no fear, lassie," she said. "It was not to warn you of your death that vision was given you. You have what is called the psychic gift, and many things will be shown you which others cannot see."

She told me that she had seen many visions, and to her, too, the Savior had appeared.

"They are well guided whom God guides," she said, "and you have nothing to fear. But," she added, "I would advise you to keep these things to yourself. Treasure them up as sacred in your own heart, for there are few who would understand them."

After this it seemed to me that I was seldom alone. I became conscious that there was with me a living presence, benignant, loving, seeking ever, it appeared to me, to guide me aright.

I began to hear strains of music that were not of this earth, but more glorious far! Often I could hear voices, thousands of them, it seemed to me, singing songs of praise and blending with the notes of some mighty celestial organ. At times it would sound loud and clear, as though close at hand, and then it would gradually diminish in volume, as though receding far off, until it was scarcely audible. And then it would swell again, resonant, jubilant, triumphant. I heard this heavenly music, for so I always regarded it, at all sorts of times and in all sorts of places —by day and by night, when alone or with others, in the house or out of doors. This music I have heard at intervals ever since.

I told my brother and a few friends in whom I could confide without bringing ridicule upon me, of the wonderful music that I heard, but even when it sounded loudest and clearest in my ears, none of them could hear it. It is in the impression it conveys of joyousness that it differs most from human music. No earthly music that I have ever heard is half so gladsome. Listening to it, one feels that it expresses a state of happiness, of faith in divine love, that is seldom if ever realized here. And always when I hear this music it is accompanied by that same exhilarating fragrance that pervaded the room wherein I beheld my first vision.

Until I was nearly eighteen no other vision came to me. Meanwhile, except for hearing the glad music of unseen voices and instruments, and the sense of a protecting presence ever near me, my life was that of most healthy, high-spirited girls in comfortable circumstances. Very happy I was in those days. My friends bestowed upon me the nickname of "Cheery."

I woke one night out of a sound sleep to find the room filled with light, although there was no light burning in it, and standing by my bedside was my dearest girl friend, Maggie.

16

Addressing me by name she said: "I have a secret to tell you. I know that I am going over to the other world before long and I want you to be with me at the last and help to comfort my mother when I am gone."

Before I had sufficiently recovered from my fear and amazement to make any response she vanished and the light slowly faded from the room.

I told the dear old Scotch lady what I had seen.

"Trust to the guidance which you will receive," she said. "If Maggie is to die in your arms, without your seeking, matters will be so arranged that you will be with her at the last."

A week later I was summoned to my friend's home. I found her suffering from a feverish cold, but there was nothing in her condition to cause alarm. She had no presentiment of impending death. And it was obvious to me that she had no remembrance of the visit she had paid me in her spirit form. Therein lies a mystery of which I can suggest no explanation. In the course of my life, I have seen several apparitions of people who were still living on the earth-plane of existence. To some of them I have spoken, and some of them have spoken to me; but subsequently I have always found that they themselves, in the body, had no knowledge or remembrance of such communications with me.

Maggie's mother was called away to see a sister living at some distance who was seriously ill, and she asked me to stay with her daughter while she was absent. I had been with

Maggie only three or four days when, one night, she was suddenly taken very ill. She expired in my arms before the doctor who had been summoned could reach her.

It was the first death that I had witnessed. Immediately after her heart had ceased to beat, I distinctly saw something in appearance like smoke, or steam as it rises from a kettle in which the water is boiling, ascend from her body. This emanation rose only a little distance and there resolved itself into a form like that of my friend who had just died. This form, shadowy at first, gradually changed until it became well defined and clad in a pearly white, cloud-like robe, beneath which the outlines of the figure were distinctly visible. The face was that of my friend but glorified, with no trace upon it of the spasm of pain which had seized her just before she died.

After I became a professional nurse, a vocation which I followed for some twenty years, I witnessed scores of deaths. And always, immediately afterwards, I saw the spirit form, in appearance an etherealized duplicate of the human form, take shape above the body in which life had become extinct, and then vanish from my sight.

TWO

When I was twenty years old my father returned from India, bought a beautiful little place in Ireland and there settled down. As a child of three I had parted from him in India, after my mother's death there. But though seventeen years had elapsed since I had seen him, it was not as strangers that we met. He had long been the hero of my girlish dreams, and in him these dreams were more than realized. Dearly I loved him and that love he returned in full measure. We were constantly together and were the best of friends and companions. My brother, too, was all that a brother could be. For two years my cup of happiness seemed filled to the brim.

Meanwhile, more acute grew the feeling of someone, unseen, tender, loving, protecting, ever with me. So close, so real did this presence seem to me at times that often I fancied I could feel a breath upon my cheek and hear a whisper at my ear, and I would turn sharply around, fully expecting to see someone. Then there came a change. I became possessed of a feeling that something dreadful was going to happen to my father. This oppressive sense of impending disaster was strongest upon me when I was most keenly conscious of the presence of my unseen mentor. It seemed to me then that someone was striving to prepare me for an ordeal which could not be averted. But my father appeared to be in his usual health and buoyant spirits. There was nothing apparent to justify my anxiety concerning him.

Some three or four weeks after this dread foreboding had come to me, I was sitting one night before the open window of my bedroom, inhaling the cool, exhilarating October air and enjoying the serene majesty of the night. Suddenly I heard my father's voice calling me by name and bidding me come to him. Then I lost all consciousness of my surroundings and a vision came to me. I saw my father lying in the garden, fully dressed and seemingly asleep. It was broad daylight. Along the road two friends were approaching the house. They were Dr. ——, our family physician, and his brother. They were in the habit of dropping in at odd times.

I saw them enter the garden gate and then, apparently catching sight of my father, run to him. One of them raised his head, and the other, the doctor, unfastened his collar and necktie and thrust a hand into his breast.

"He has gone," I heard the doctor say. "He must have passed away without a moment's pain. But who will tell his daughter? I cannot!"

Then the vision vanished and I became aware that I was still sitting at the open window. I lit a lamp and went to my father's bedroom, gently opened the door, and listened. I heard the deep, regular breathing that denotes sound slumber. I entered the room and walked softly to the bedside. I knelt there and prayed fervently that my father might be spared to me. But it was with a heart as heavy as when I entered the room that I left it, so strong was my conviction that that which I had seen in the vision would soon come to pass.

I did not return to bed that night, for the dread fear that possessed me had banished all possibility of sleep; but it was with a smile that I greeted my father at the breakfast table next morning, for I was resolved that no shadow of my anxiety and despair should fall upon him. And he was as cheerful, tender, loving and companionable as he had always been.

He left the house at two o'clock that afternoon for a walk, telling me he would be back at four to take tea with me. Before going he kissed me affectionately, as he always did when leaving me, even for a short time; but I felt that never again on earth should I receive a kiss from those dear lips. I betook myself to my room to await the blow that I knew was soon to fall.

About half-past three a man-servant came in hastily and asked me if I knew where "the master" was. A little later the other man-servant asked me the same question. Then the stable-man of a military friend came in, looking troubled and asked me if "the master" had come in, adding that Captain —— wanted to see him.

I was convinced that what I had seen in the vision had befallen; that my father was already dead and these men knew it, but were afraid to tell me.

"My father has not returned," I answered, "but why do you look so alarmed, Andrew? Have you any bad news to tell me?"

"No, miss," he replied, with downcast eyes, and hurried away.

He had been only a little while gone when Dr. —— came in. The moment I saw his face I knew that he had brought with him a message of death, but feared to tell it to me. I thought that I would make the telling of it easier for him.

"You have come to tell me that my father has met with an accident, or worse—that he is dead," I said.

"He has been badly hurt," he answered, "and—and they are bringing him in."

"Why not tell me the truth now, Doctor?" I said. "I know that my father has passed away."

"I must not deny it to you," he answered, falteringly. "He is dead."

22

In a few minutes my dear father's lifeless body was brought in.

After the funeral, Dr. —— asked me what had made me so positive, before I had been told of it, that my father was dead. Then I told him of the vision I had seen. I learned from him that all I had seen in the vision had actually occurred; that he and his brother had done just what I had seen them do; that he had spoken the very words that I had heard him speak.

My father had died of heart disease. It was not until after his death I learned that for two years previously he had known of his ailment, and that at any moment he might be stricken dead. But, like the gallant soldier he was, and with the same calm courage that had carried him through all the horrors of the Indian Mutiny, he had received his death sentence, and had hidden all knowledge of it from his children that it might not mar their happiness.

THREE

After the loss of my father black despair settled on my soul. My feelings seemed to be petrified. Even the relief of tears was denied me. I hardened my heart against God. I said: "God would never have been so cruel as to take my father from me; therefore there is no God." I ceased going to church and abandoned myself to the gloomiest thoughts. Their hold upon me was strengthened by other sorrows and troubles which followed fast. After my father's death it was found that the supposed friend to whom he had entrusted the investment of his money had misappropriated it and there was nothing left for his children. My brother, resolved to make a living for both of us, went to a British colony and was there drowned. My favorite aunt died. I had a nervous breakdown, followed by a long illness. Convinced that life held nothing for me that could make it worth living, I rejected all efforts to give me solace and comfort.

About two years after my father's death an uncle with whom I was then living persuaded me to accompany him on a visit to a relative who was the matron of a large hospital. He hoped that it might lead to my taking up nursing as a profession, for unless I could be induced to take an interest in something that would turn my thoughts from myself he was convinced that I should never regain my health.

The matron gave me permission to spend part of each day in the wards. Then I began to observe the work of the nurses; to note with what skill, tenderness and patience they ministered to those placed under their care, and how often they succeeded in relieving their sufferings. I fell to contrasting my life, burdensome to myself and contributing nothing to the happiness of anybody, with the lives of these nurses. The desire came upon me that I, too, could do such work, but I felt utterly unfitted for it, unworthy of it and incapable of ridding myself of the gloomy thoughts, centered in self, that had become habitual with me.

A few weeks after my first visit to the hospital I left it one morning, feeling that I could no longer endure such a useless, unhappy life as mine had become, and resolved to find some

26

way of escape from it. I wandered about aimlessly for hours, sitting down now and again when I could find a seat, and debating with myself the justifiability of suicide. As time went on the case for suicide grew stronger in my mind; that for life weaker. At last I was convinced that the best thing I could do, both for myself and for those whose misfortune it was to be bound to me by the ties of relationship, was to kill myself. There only remained for me to decide what means I should adopt.

While running over in my mind the various ways open to me by which I could end the life that had become hateful to me, and trying to decide which of them I should take, I heard the refrain of an old familiar hymn. Then I saw that I was passing a church. Something which I seemed powerless to resist impelled me to go in. It was the first house of worship I had entered since my father's death.

The hymn they were singing there was "Jesus, Lover of my soul." It had been my father's favorite hymn, and often I had sung it to him in the happy days that now seemed long years behind me. The words and the music touched some spring of emotion that I had thought was dead within me, and sinking into the nearest seat I buried my face in my hands and gave way to a flood of tears.

After a time, I know not how long, I became aware that the service was over and that I was kneeling alone in the church, now dimly illumined by a few gas jets. Something like the calm that often succeeds the tempest had fallen on my storm-swept soul.

I raised my head and looked up, and for the second time found myself gazing at the white-robed figure of the Savior, surrounded by a bright light, which seemed to emanate from His own person. For a short time I gazed, spellbound by the indescribably tender passion depicted on that radiant face.

"Oh, help me!" I cried, "for I am afraid to live and yet I dare not die."

The Savior stretched forth His hands in a gesture of loving appeal, and said in tones that revealed a depth of sympathy and tenderness no human voice is capable of expressing:

"Come unto Me, weary one and stricken with despair, and I will comfort you and give you work to do for Me. Now go in peace."

The vision faded from my sight. A great burden seemed lifted from my soul, and I left the church resolved to begin a new life, a life that should be of some use to others.

I have no recollection how I reached the house in which I was staying, but late that night I came to myself to find the good matron bending over me while I lay on the bed, fully dressed. She was alarmed by my appearance and summoned my uncle. I told him what I had seen.

"Thank God!" he exclaimed fervently. "This will be a turning point in your life."

FOUR

The unhappy life—the life which I seemed to have been living so long, though it had really lasted only a little more than two years—appeared to have fallen from me. My thoughts, which had been centered on my own grief and wretchedness, began to flow into new channels. Vistas of another life—a life that should be of some benefit to others—opened up before me.

Again I was able to pray; again I was able to yield myself to the gentle influence of my unseen mentor. And like the strains of some haunting melody again and again there recurred to me those words: "I will comfort you and give you work to do for Me."

That work lay close at hand. I was admitted to the hospital as a probationer. With zest I applied myself to the duties assigned to me, and in striving to assuage the sufferings of others found the boon of self-forgetfulness. More real to me became the presence of my invisible guardian and keener my susceptibility to the tender guidance. Often I was conscious of being helped thereby to perform tasks which seemed beyond my own physical strength, and of being prevented making mistakes in my eagerness to help some poor sufferer. It seemed as though at times an impetuous movement was checked by a restraining hand laid on mine. At other times a voice seemed to whisper at my ear: "Nay, do not do that: do this," and I would immediately become aware of what was the proper thing to do and how it should be done.

There are some phases of hospital work of which the casual visitor who sees only the patients lying in scrupulously clean and neat little cots, knows nothing. Some of the sights a nurse sees and some of the things she has to do are too revolting to bear description. It was about three months after I had joined the hospital that I was first brought into sharp contact with this ugly side of the work of a hospital nurse. At the spectacle laid bare to me of the hideous ravages wrought by a disease caused by depravity and vice, I was filled with loathing and a sensation of physical nausea. I turned from the patient in disgust. "I will not—I cannot—defile myself by touching this man," I said to myself.

Then a flood of light descended upon me and, looking upwards, I beheld, bending over the patient, the figure of the Savior. He turned His head and looked down on me, and stretching forth His hands over the disease-disfigured sinner, said:

"Inasmuch as ye do it unto these ye do it unto Me. In every creature entrusted to your care behold Me and the work will be easy."

The vision—if vision it were—vanished. I turned again to the patient. Gone was all the loathing and disgust which I had felt a few moments before.

Such pitiable cases came under my care in the course of my hospital experience. And always when called upon to minister to these victims of their own sinful lives there recurred to me the words, "Inasmuch as ye do it unto these ye do it unto Me," and the work was made easy.

The duties of a nurse are often arduous and exacting; but throughout the years that I earned my livelihood as a nurse, whenever overcome by fatigue, depression or physical weakness, nearly always I was able to gain renewed strength, courage and hope by recalling this vision of the Savior and the words that fell from His lips.

FIVE

At the time the man who had made such a woeful moral and physical wreck of his life was under my care, there was admitted to the hospital a young boy whose thigh had been broken in an accident. He was not under my charge, but I was greatly drawn to him, for he had one of the sweetest natures I have ever known in a child, and he bore excruciating pain with extraordinary fortitude. Once he said to me: "I shall be so glad when the time comes for me to go away from all this suffering. My father is waiting for me to come to him."

"Where is your father, child?" I asked.

"He is up in the sky with the angels," he answered, with a

smile on his wan little face. "The angels took him away and I shall be glad when the time comes for them to take me to him, for I love him best."

That same night I was standing by the child's bedside when I became conscious of a dark, shadowy form standing at the foot of the bed. Looking at it intently, I perceived that the form was like that of a human being, but dimly visible, as a man or woman appears seen through a thick fog. It was enveloped in a long robe and its features were veiled. I stretched out my hand to touch it, but could feel nothing, although I could see that it was still there. A moment later it vanished.

A feeling of dread came over me and I could not shake off the impression that the apparition portended something dire. Ere the morning dawned, as I learned next day, the child died.

Afterwards I often saw the dark, veiled form standing at the foot of a bed in which lay some patient whose condition was critical. I came in time to recognize that it portended the speedy death of the patient at the foot of whose bed it appeared, for it was always there it stood. Never since it first appeared to me, has anybody died who has been in my care, whether at the hospital or in private houses where I have been engaged as a nurse, that it has not appeared to me before the death occurred. And generally the death has followed within two or three days after its appearance.

But it was not long after I had first seen the dark, veiled form in the hospital that another apparition appeared to me, in every way presenting a striking contrast to the veiled one.

34

It was a bright figure, clad in a cloud-like, luminous robe and with a youthful face of joyous aspect. It first appeared to me when I was watching by the bedside of a patient whose condition was very serious. It stood at the head of the bed with the right arm upraised and the index finger pointing upward, the gesture and expression indicative of hope. That was the feeling with which it inspired me. All my fears for the patient were dispelled. His condition immediately began to improve and he soon recovered.

After this the bright form appeared to me often, invariably in the same place at the head of a patient's bed, and always the gesture and expression were the same.

As I came to regard the dark form as the harbinger of death, so, after repeatedly noting that the patient always got better by whose bed I had seen the bright form appear, I came to regard the latter as the harbinger of renewed life. I do not mean by this that I considered its appearance constituted a positive assurance that the patient would recover under any circumstances and quite independent of any human agency. The message which it seemed always to convey to me was, "Hope —and work." Its effect upon me was to make me strive all the harder to do what lay in my power to assist the patient's recovery.

In all my experience as a nurse I never knew a patient to die with whom I had seen the radiant figure. It must not be inferred from this that in every instance the recovery of a patient in my care was preceded by its appearance. It appeared only when the patient's condition denoted serious danger. With those who were suffering from ailments or accidents that were not dangerous—and such, happily, constitute the majority of those who undergo hospital treatment—their recovery, when under my care, was not preceded by the appearance of the bright one. But always, as I have stated, when any one died who was in my care, the death was preceded by the appearance of the dark veiled form. Neither the best surgical or medical skill, nor the most conscientious and devoted nursing, ever availed to save one by whose bedside I had seen it.

I never told any of the doctors or nurses in the hospital what it was that made me so sure certain patients would recover and that certain other patients would die, because I was convinced they would not believe that I could really see what they could not see; but as time went on in the hospital—and always my predictions of recovery or death were verified—it came to be generally recognized among the nurses, and to some extent among the doctors, that I possessed some weird gift which enabled me to foretell such things.

Often I was asked by other nurses who had serious cases in their care to look at their patients and tell them what I thought of their chances of recovery. Sometimes as I stood by their beds the dark, veiled form would appear, and sometimes the radiant form, and my opinion would be given accordingly. But often neither would appear, and then I would venture no opinion.

36

SIX

In the hospital I became familiar with death. I saw some
die who welcomed death gladly as the deliverer from pain,
grief, weariness and care; as the opener of the door through
which, released from all physical infirmities, their spirits
would pass to a broader, freer sphere of existence where they
would realize the deepest longings of their souls. Others I saw
die who, overcome by physical weakness and mental weariness,
seemed incapable of either hope or fear, and awaited death
utterly indifferent as to what might follow.

I witnessed some deaths that were calm and peaceful and
as good to look upon as the falling asleep of a babe. And some

I saw in which physical agony persisted until the last gasp, and they were dreadful to see. Still more appalling were the deaths of those who, realizing that their end was near, were terror-stricken by the fear of what might befall them afterwards and fought for life, clung to it, begged and prayed that they might be allowed to live. Happily such scenes were rare. Most of those whom I saw die passed away in a state of torpor, incapable, seemingly, of feeling or expressing any emotion.

But I noticed that often, irrespective of the physical condition or frame of mind of the dying, just before the end came they would seem to recognize some one who was not of those at the bedside and was by the latter unseen. I have seen a woman who had been in a comatose state for hours, suddenly open her eyes with a look of glad surprise, stretch forth her hands as though to grasp invisible hands outstretched towards her, and then, with what seemed a sigh of relief, expire. I have seen a man who had been writhing in agony suddenly grow calm, fasten his eyes with an expression of joyful recognition on what to those observing him was only vacancy, and uttering a name in tones of glad greeting, breathe his last breath.

I recall the death of a woman who was the victim of that most dreadful disease, malignant cancer. Her sufferings were excruciating, and she prayed earnestly that death might speedily come to her and end her agony. Suddenly her sufferings appeared to cease; the expression of her face, which a moment before had been distorted by pain, changed to one of radiant joy. Gazing upwards, with a glad light in her eyes, she raised her hands and exclaimed: "Oh, mother dear, you have come to take me home. I am so glad!" And in another moment her physical life had ceased.

The memory of another death which occurred about the same time comes back to me. It was that of an old soldier who was in the last stages of tuberculosis, brought on by exposure while fighting his country's battles. He was brave and patient but had frequent paroxysms of pain that were almost unendurable, and he longed for the relief which he knew death alone could bring him. One of these spasms had seized upon him, and his features were convulsed with agony as he fought for breath, when he suddenly grew calm. A smile lit up his face, and, looking upwards, he exclaimed, with a ring of joy in his voice, "Marion, my daughter!" Then the end came.

His brother and sister were at the bedside. The sister said to the brother: "He saw Marion, his favorite daughter. She came and took him where he will suffer no more." And she added fervently: "Thank God! he has found rest at last."

That at such moments as I have described the dying really see some spirit form—some one who has come from the other world to welcome them on their birth into the new life—I never doubted. And the time came when, as will be told later, it was revealed to me that this is what they really do see. It is not, as some suppose, a phantom creation of their own imagina-

39

tion on which they gaze so gladly just before death occurs, but a ministering spirit—an angel—and more highly endowed with life and vitality than are those who have not yet undergone the change wrought by death.

But whether the deaths I witnessed were peaceful or painful, preceded or not preceded by the recognition of some one from the other world, always, immediately after the physical life had ceased, I saw the spirit form take shape above the dead body, in appearance a glorified replica of it. However painful might have been the last hours, however protracted and wasting the illness, no trace of suffering or disease appeared upon the radiant spirit face. Striking, at times, was the contrast which it presented to the human features, pain-distorted and deep-furrowed by suffering.

Often I have longed to tell the weeping ones at the bedside what I had seen, but I seldom did so because I felt they would not believe that it was possible I could have seen that which was invisible to them. Ardently I have wished at such times that they, too, could have beheld the etherealized form of the one they mourned and have carried away from the death chamber, stamped forever on their memories, the picture of the radiant spirit face. One glimpse of it would have robbed death of much of its sting. And sometimes, I am sure, it would have turned mourning into rejoicing.

SEVEN

It was about six months after I began to work in the hospital that it was revealed to me that the dying often really do see those who have come from the realms of spirit life to welcome them on their entrance into another state of existence.

The first time that I received this ocular proof was at the death of L——, a sweet girl of seventeen, who was a personal friend of mine. She was a victim of consumption. She suffered no pain, but the weariness that comes from extreme weakness and debility was heavy upon her and she yearned for rest.

A short time before she expired I became aware that two spirit forms were standing by the bedside, one on either side of it. I did not see them enter the room; they were standing by the bedside when they first became visible to me, but I could see them as distinctly as I could any of the human occupants of the room. In my own thoughts I have always called these bright beings from another world, angels, and as such I shall hereafter speak of them. I recognized their faces as those of two girls who had been the closest friends of the girl who was dying. They had passed away a year before and were then about her own age.

Just before they appeared the dying girl exclaimed: "It has grown suddenly dark; I cannot see anything!" But she recognized them immediately. A smile, beautiful to see, lit up her face. She stretched forth her hands and in joyous tones exclaimed: "Oh, you have come to take me away! I am glad, for I am very tired."

As she stretched forth her hands the two angels extended each a hand, one grasping the dying girl's right hand; the other her left hand. Their faces were illumined by a smile more radiantly beautiful even than that of the face of the girl who was so soon to find the rest for which she longed. She did not speak again, but for nearly a minute her hands remained outstretched, grasped by the hands of the angels, and she continued to gaze at them with the glad light in her eyes and the smile on her face.

Her father, mother and brother, who had been summoned that they might be present when the end came, began to weep bitterly, for they knew that she was leaving them. From my

42

heart there went up a prayer that they might see what I saw, but they could not.

The angels seemed to relax their grasp of the girl's hands, which then fell back on the bed. A sigh came from her lips, such as one might give who resigns himself gladly to a much needed sleep, and in another moment she was what the world calls dead. But that sweet smile with which she had first recognized the angels was still stamped on her features.

The two angels remained by the bedside during the brief space that elapsed before the spirit form took shape above the body in which the physical life had ceased. Then they rose and stood for a few moments one on each side of her, who was now like unto themselves. And three angels went from the room where, a short time before, there had been only two.

When the weeping relatives had withdrawn from the room I went to the window, and threw it wide open and gazed out into the night, wondering whither the angels had gone and longing that I, too, might go there. Then I heard a voice, melodious but authoritative. And the words, which I heard as distinctly as I have ever heard words uttered by a human voice, were: "Not yet; your work on earth is not yet finished."

Often, often, in the years that were to come, did I see angels depart with a new-born angel in their care, and nearly always did the same longing come to me that I might join them. And many times did that same voice say to me: "Not yet; your work on earth is not yet finished."

I could do little to assuage the grief of the father, mother and brother of the girl whose death had brought me such absolute assurance that she had joined the angels in a happier state of existence than is found on earth. I dared not tell them what I had seen. They would not have believed that I could have seen what they had not seen. Least of all would the father have credited it. He was a good man but he was an atheist, and he had convinced himself that there was no future life. His daughter's last words, the smile that lit up her face as she recognized the angels who had come to take her spirit away, he regarded as evidence only of a disordered imagination. In fact he told me as much. I did not even attempt to persuade him that he was mistaken, for I knew that it would have been useless. But I felt very sorry for him, for he would permit no ray of hope that in another life he might meet his dearly loved daughter to penetrate the deep gloom of his sorrow. The mother and brother had this hope and their grief was not so bitter.

EIGHT

There are many, happily, who, although they cannot themselves see the angels whom the dying often recognize so joyfully, believe that they are really ministering spirits, come to welcome those who, through the portals of death, are about to enter the eternal life.

About a month after the death of the girl which is related in the preceding chapter, another friend of mine died in the hospital. It was pneumonia that carried him off. He was a good and devout man and for him death held no terrors, for he was sure that it was but the transition to a happier, more exalted life than can be lived here. His only regret at dying was that he would leave behind him a dearly-loved wife; but that regret was softened by the assurance that their parting would be only for a time, and that she would join him some day in that other world whither he was going.

She was sitting by his bed and, believing as he believed, was awaiting the end with resignation. About an hour before he died he called her by name and pointing upwards, said: "Look, L——, there is B——! He is waiting for me. And now he smiles and holds out his hands to me. Can't you see him?"

"No, dear, I cannot see him," she replied, "but I know that he is there because you see him."

B—— was their only child who had been taken from them about a year before, when between five and six years of age. I could plainly see the little angel with curly flaxen hair and blue eyes, and garbed in what I call the spirit robe. The face was just that of a winsome child, but etherealized and radiant as no earthly faces ever are.

The father had been greatly weakened by the ravages of his disease and the joyful emotion occasioned by seeing his angel child seemed to exhaust what little vitality he had left. He closed his eyes and sank into a placid sleep. He remained in that state for about an hour, the angel child meanwhile staying poised above the bed with an expression of glad expectancy on his radiant face. Occasionally he looked lovingly at his mother.

The breathing of the dying man grew fainter and fainter until it ceased altogether. Then again I witnessed what had now

46

become a familiar spectacle to me—the formation of the spirit body above the discarded earthly body. When it was complete the angel child clasped the hand of the now angel father, each gazed into the eyes of the other with an expression of the tenderest affection, and with faces aglow with joy and happiness they vanished.

It was, indeed, a glorious sight! It made death, which nearly everybody regards as something awesome, enshrouded in dark, impenetrable mystery, appear beautiful and beneficent, indeed as the crowning proof of the infinite mercy and unfathomable love of the Heavenly Father. Had it not been for the presence of the weeping widow I could have clapped my hands and have sung for very joy. But her grief was not of the same black and bitter quality which had seized upon me when my father died and caused me to reject all solace.

"I am very glad my dear husband saw B—— before he died," she said to me that same evening. "It was natural that B—— should come for him to take him to the angels, for they loved each other dearly. I shall now be able to think of them as always together and happy. And when I receive my summons I know that they will both come for me."

After I left the hospital and devoted myself to private nursing, no patient died in my care that I did not see an angel, or two angels, waiting by the bedside to conduct the deathless soul to its new sphere of existence when its corruptible body had been exchanged for a spirit body. The angels whom I saw

47

on these occasions differed with respect to their figures and features just as much as do human beings at various stages of life, some having youthful faces; others, faces which indicated that they had lived to a ripe old age on earth.

But the faces of these angels, whether indicative of youth or old age and of whatever type, were all aglow with something that so unmistakably bespoke love, tenderness, goodness, that they were all beautiful to look upon. And though the shining faces might be patriarchal in expression, with long, flowing white beards and snowy hair, they conveyed no suggestion of the physical decay and decrepitude which usually are associated with extreme old age on earth. Whether the faces of these radiant ones indicated that they had passed from this earth life young, middle-aged or old, they were all, so they impressed me, endowed with more vigor and vitality than is ever possessed by those who still abide on this earth. In short, it seems to me, that those beings whom we speak of as dead are far more vitally alive than those who have yet to pay the great debt of nature.

Always, or nearly always, when the waiting angels were seen by the dying just before death, or by their spirits just afterwards, it seemed to me that they were recognized much as one recognizes those whom one is glad to meet on earth. This, to my mind, indicated that these angels, before they themselves underwent the transformation wrought by death, had been when on earth relations or friends of those who recognized

48

them. This was obviously so when, as in some of the scenes I have described, the dying called them by name. And as when we take ship to some far country to which we are entire strangers, our relations or friends, if we are fortunate enough to have such there, gather to greet us on landing and conduct us to our new homes; so it is natural that the first to meet us, and greet us when we cross the threshold of the other world, should be some of those who were dear to us who have preceded us there.

NINE

It is not only doctors and nurses who minister to the sick and suffering. Angels also minister to them. This, too, was revealed to me while I was at the hospital.

By the light of a shaded lamp I was writing one night at a table in the middle of the ward, of which I was in charge as night nurse. The few other lights that were burning were turned low. Glancing up from the paper on which I was writing I saw a figure moving about at one end of the long and dimly lighted room. I thought that it was some patient who had got out of her bed, but when I approached near I perceived that it was not a patient, but an angel. The figure was tall and slender, the features were those of a woman of middle age.

I had become too familiar by this time with the sudden appearance of these radiant visitors from another world to be alarmed or startled by it, however unexpected, and I stood still and watched her. She went to three or four beds, pausing for a brief space at each one of them and laying her right hand on the heads of the patients occupying them.

After this, as long as I remained at the hospital scarcely a day passed that I did not see this angel ministering to the sick. But it was when I was on night duty that I saw her oftenest; for it is in the dark hours, and especially during those that precede the dawn, that the life forces of those who are battling with disease sink lowest and they stand most in need of whatever will stimulate their vitality and ease their pain. That this angel was endowed with some power by means of which she could at times materially benefit the sick was made so abundantly evident soon after I had first seen her, that I came to call her in my thoughts the healing angel.

Thankful I was always, but especially at night, when I was usually the only nurse in the ward, to see her flitting among the patients and here and there laying her hand on the forehead of some sufferer, for I knew that the recipient of that ministry, though absolutely unconscious of it, would be benefited by it. Often, after such a treatment, has a patient said to me on awaking, "Oh, nurse, I feel so much better this morning: I have had such a refreshing sleep."

52

Occasionally patients who, I knew, had received the ministry of the healing angel, would tell me that they had had beautiful dreams in which they had heard entrancing music. I wondered sometimes if they had heard strains of the celestial music which I so often heard. But none of them apparently ever saw, as I did, the angel who had wrought the change in them for which they were so grateful.

Her healing powers were not exercised on patients only when they were asleep. I have seen her more than once lay her hand on the forehead of a patient who was suffering such acute pain that it provoked moans and groans. And a little later, relieved of the pain, the patient would sink into a calm sleep, to awaken greatly improved. Frequently, after the healing angel had paid a visit to one of my patients, I have found that the pulse had become more regular and the temperature nearer normal.

Ofttimes the healing angel helped me when I was attending a patient, sometimes guiding my hand; at other times, incredible as it may seem, she actually assisted me to raise or shift some heavy and helpless victim of disease or accident.

Apart from those other angels of whom I have written, the healing angel was not the only one I saw among the patients in the hospital. Others came and went occasionally, much as did human visitors, except that their coming and going was different—a sudden appearing and a sudden disappearing. But the healing angel was the only one of whom I am able to affirm positively, because it was proved to me repeatedly,

53

that she brought healing to the patients to whom she ministered.

A young woman who had been run over by a heavy vehicle and terribly injured internally, afforded the most convincing proof that came under my notice of the efficacy of the healing angel's ministrations. She was placed in a ward in which I was on night duty. After making a thorough examination of her, the doctor in charge had pronounced her case hopeless.

She had been in the ward only a short time and I was standing by her bed, wondering what I could do to alleviate her sufferings, which were great, and thinking how sad it was that her two little children should so soon be deprived of a mother's love and care, when the bright angel appeared at the head of the bed with uplifted hand, pointing upwards. Brief, as always, was his stay, but it caused my despondency to give way to hope, although it still seemed to me that nothing short of a miracle could keep life in that dreadfully shattered body.

About an hour later I was applying cool, damp cloths to her forehead when I saw the healing angel at the opposite side of the bed. She put forth her right hand and laid it for a moment on the hand with which I was holding the cloth against the sufferer's brow. There was something very soothing in her touch, and so gentle was it, I might say that I "sensed" it rather than felt it. As she withdrew her hand she raised her head and looked into my eyes. It was not a beautiful face that confronted me, judged by the ordinary standards of beauty, but there was stamped upon it a sweetness and tenderness that was far more attractive than mere beauty.

54

"Be of good cheer," she said, "she will recover."

It was the first time that the healing angel had spoken to me, but often afterwards when she was ministering to my patients she spoke to me words of similar hopeful import.

That night she came several times to the woman's bedside, each time laying her right hand on the patient's brow, but up to the time that I went off duty, at nine o'clock in the morning, there had been no perceptible change in the patient's condition. The following night the healing angel again paid several visits to the sufferer, and she had some refreshing sleep, but when the doctor saw her before I went off duty again he was still convinced that her case was hopeless.

While he was talking to me about it the healing angel appeared, standing very near us. Though as plainly visible to me as was the doctor himself, I knew that he could not see her. As he again expressed the opinion that the woman could not recover, the angel gave me a sweet smile of reassurance. Emboldened by it, I said to the doctor:

"The case does look hopeless as far as we can see, but still I believe that she will recover."

"Nonsense, nurse," he replied; "it is impossible that she should pull through after such terrible injuries as she has received. But," he added, "we shall, of course, do everything that it is possible to do for her."

That night there occurred a quite perceptible improvement in her condition, and her temperature, which had been very high, was lowered.

55

"Yes, she does seem a little better," said the doctor in the morning. "But it can only be a temporary improvement."

Night after night the healing angel continued to minister to her, and some weeks after she had been admitted to the hospital she was able to return to her home. She was not as strong and sound as she had been before the accident—I don't know that she ever recovered to that extent—but she was able to attend to her household duties and give her children the love and care they needed. It was regarded in the hospital as a wonderful recovery.

"I never thought to see her on her feet again," said the doctor who had repeatedly pronounced her case utterly hopeless. "I look upon her recovery as simply miraculous."

TEN

While a staff nurse at the hospital I had to take my turn at what the nurses called "extern" duty, that is work outside the hospital. It consisted in attending at their homes to the pressing needs of those who were too poor to be able to pay for such service. When to the grievous burden imposed by dire poverty are added those caused by pain and disease, the depths of human misery are reached. It makes me shudder, even now, to recall some of the many pitiful scenes I have witnessed as a nurse among the dwellers in the slums. I have seen a man dying on a filthy pallet in one corner of a room, while in another corner, on an equally wretched makeshift for

57

a bed, a woman gave birth to a child. And this was in a Christian land!

But my purpose in this book is to relate only those experiences which have given me some knowledge of the ministry of the angels.

N—— was a man who had been reared in affluence, had received a University education and had moved in good society. But his father lost his entire fortune in some financial crash just before his death, and instead of leaving his son well provided for, as he had expected to do, left him penniless and very ill-equipped for the struggle for a livelihood.

He was at the time engaged to a young lady of excellent family. He broke off the engagement because he loved her too well to ask her to share his poverty with him. Too proud to accept what he would have regarded as alms, he hid himself from those who had known him in his prosperous days and set manfully to work to earn his own living. In his straitened circumstances he could not seek far for employment and took a situation as a clerk in a retail linen-draper's shop. He did not acquaint the woman whom he loved with his address because he believed that it would be best for her, in the long run, that she should think that he had become indifferent to her and thereby be helped to forget him. But by chance she discovered him in the shop where he was employed. And she, a high-souled, unselfish character, persuaded him that she would be far happier sharing his poverty than she could be living in comfortable circumstances apart from him.

They were married and started housekeeping in two small rooms in a tenement. Unfortunately she was not physically strong. His small salary scarcely sufficed to provide the bare necessities of life. She fell ill. The doctor had to be called in. Among other things, he prescribed for his patient a more nourishing diet than N—— could afford out of his wretched pittance. His hours of employment were long, but he tried, by working extra hours at anything he could get to do, to add something to his slender income.

Still he did not make enough to provide for his wife what the delicate state of her health imperatively demanded. She grew worse. In his desperation he forged a check for a few pounds. That money, too, soon went. He could not bring himself to forge another check, for he was tortured by the thought that by the crime he had committed he had erected a moral barrier between himself and his wife; and although it was for her sake he had done it, he had rendered himself thereby unworthy of her love.

The approach of the time when the advent of a little stranger was to be expected made the outlook for them still more distressing. It was at this juncture that the doctor who was attending the wife notified the hospital of the state of affairs, and I was sent to the wretched home to nurse the poor lady. Gradually I learned the pitiful story, of which I have given an outline.

I have seen much of sorrow, hardship and misery, but never anything, I think, which so moved my heart to pity as the lot

59

of poor N—— and his wife. If anything, N——'s ordeal was the more trying. He had to contend with the bitter knowledge that it was because of his own inability to provide for his wife's needs that she had been brought so low in health. And to this was added the torture of remorse for the forgery he had committed, which was intensified, rather than lessened, by the fact that it had not been detected and no expiation had been exacted of him.

Through it all he strove to be cheerful for his wife's sake. Though he never told me so, I know that he often went hungry that he might buy some little delicacy for her. She, too, strove always to be cheerful for her husband's sake and bore her sufferings uncomplainingly. "I am sure I shall be better tomorrow," she would tell him with a pathetic smile when he asked her how she felt.

But her feeble strength continued to wane and one night I saw at the foot of her bed the dark figure with the veiled face. Then I knew that her end was very near. But knowing, too, the glorious new birth and the instant release from all pain, weariness and weakness that was in store for her, it was with a feeling of relief, as far as she was concerned, that I awaited her death. It was the thought of how her husband's heart would be racked that filled me with anxiety.

The baby was born dead and the mother soon followed it into the better world. Then did I see that which I think is more painful to witness than the most excruciating of physical suf-

fering—the agony of a soul. It was laid absolutely bare to
me. N—— accused himself of being the author of his wife's
death. But for him, he declared, she would still be living in
comfort and happiness. Because he had been too much of a
coward to fight the battle against poverty alone, he had ac-
cepted her offer to share it with him, and thereby he had
brought death upon her. He had committed forgery: he had
proved himself the most abject and contemptible of failures.

Then came upon him the realization of his own desolation.
How could he bear to endure what might remain to him of
life deprived of the companionship of her whom he loved so
fondly? He could not. He would rid himself of life that held
only misery for him by committing suicide.

From my own experience I knew something of what his
feelings were, and from my own experience I knew, too, how
futile it would be to attempt to comfort him by such consola-
tory thoughts as are sanctioned by orthodox religion.

Tell him that his wife had gone to a far-off heaven, where
she was peaceful and happy! Where, *perhaps,* they might some
day meet and recognize each other! Where, *perhaps,* they
might find the ties of love which had bound them on earth
still persisted!

I knew what it was that filled him with black despair and
made life appear insupportable to him. It was the thought that
through all the long years that he might be destined to live on
earth, if he did not himself cut short his life, he would be de-

61

prived of his wife's love, sympathy and companionship; that all that time no thought, no tender message from her, could ever penetrate the invisible barrier that separated them and reach his hungry heart! Religion had taught him much that had helped him to do his duty, nobly and unselfishly, but it had given him no ground to hope that the solace for which he yearned—for which every heart cries out under similar circumstances—might be granted him.

Something seemed to say to me, "Tell him a little of what you know of the angels and their ministry. He will believe."

I told him how I had seen the glorified spirit form of his wife above her worn-out, earthly body. I told him that the so-called dead were often able to return to their loved ones on earth. I told him that I had often seen angels ministering to human beings. And I told him that though by suicide he would gain entrance to another state of existence, it would not be that blessed sphere where his wife had found her home; that after committing self-murder it might require long, long years of expiation before he could attain to her exalted state.

"If I could realize her presence and companionship at times," he said, "if I knew that her loving thoughts could still reach me, I could bear to live on."

All that he might realize, I assured him; but he would first have to regain his trust in God; by prayer he would have to rid himself of the dark and bitter thoughts that now possessed him and open the windows of his soul to the light of

62

divine love. And then, when alone, he might become conscious of the presence of his angel wife and receive thought messages from her, which, though not uttered in words that to him would be audible, would be clearly intelligible to his soul.

Before I left him he had abandoned all thought of suicide. What I had told him had implanted in him the hope that what remained to him of life would not be passed in that utter loneliness and desolation which he had believed inevitable. Only a few days later he told me that he had been able to realize the presence of his wife; that she had spoken to his soul that which brought him peace and comfort.

But the great strain to which he had been subjected, coupled with prolonged overwork, brought upon him a nervous breakdown. Then, for a time, he was under my care as a nurse. Frequently when attending him I saw his wife by his bedside ministering to him. He could not see her as I did—how I wished that he could!—but he told me that he could "feel" her presence.

He recovered and for some time I was able to keep in touch with him. More and more he came to realize the frequent presence and companionship of his wife. And not only, he told me, did he receive from her assurances of her love and sympathy, but she conveyed to him holy and uplifting thoughts of God's infinite love and mercy, whereby he was able to attain to a trust in God deeper and more abiding than he had known when his dearly loved wife was visibly sharing his life.

He paid back anonymously the money he had obtained by means of the forged check. He helped others in distress by counsel, sympathy and kindness, and by money, too, when he could afford it. Many were made better by knowing him.

When his wife died it had seemed to him impossible that he could be anything but a miserable, broken-hearted man if he continued to live. From that fate he had been saved by the discovery that death had not separated his wife from him; that as an angel she could return to him, comfort and cheer him and strengthen his trust in God.

ELEVEN

Many persons, unknown to themselves, are endowed, I believe, with some form of what are commonly called psychic powers, by means of which, when these powers are developed, they can hold communion with those who through death have passed to another state of existence. Some may be able at times to see them; others, to hear them; and some favored ones may both see and hear them. Others again, though they may be unable ever either to see or hear them, are susceptible to their influence. Indeed, I believe that the great majority of people are thus influenced, though comparatively few are aware of it. And susceptibility to spirit influence may be cultivated and developed until it becomes one of the greatest of blessings.

After I had left the hospital and taken up private nursing I was engaged to nurse an old lady who was suffering from a painful internal disease, incurable save through an operation, which at her advanced age would have proved fatal. She was a widow and her only daughter lived with her. She bore her sufferings with great fortitude, never complaining, but the grief of the daughter when she learned that her mother would soon be taken from her was heart-rending.

The daughter was a good and devout woman. She believed that her mother would find rest and happiness in heaven. It was the thought of how lonely she herself would be when the one she loved so dearly had gone from her, coupled with the conviction, which was almost part of her religious faith, that between her mother in heaven and herself on earth communication would be impossible, that made her so dread the life that lay before her.

I tried to convince her that such communication was possible by telling her of some of the instances I had witnessed of angel ministry; but her own deep religious convictions stood in the way of her acceptance of my statements as facts.

"I would love to believe as you do," she said, "but I cannot. If the dead can at times return to earth and communicate with the living, surely some of our religious teachers would know of it and would tell us of it. It is too good to be true. We are not fit to be visited and comforted by angels."

66

The time came when the end was very near. The mother had been for some time unconscious and the daughter was kneeling by the bedside, weeping, her face buried in her hands. Suddenly two angels became visible to me, standing on either side of the bed. The face of one was that of a man who, when he departed from this life, was apparently about sixty years of age. His beard and hair were iron-gray. But there was stamped on his features that indescribable something indicative of exuberant vitality and vigor, which shines forth from all angel faces I have seen, whether in other respects they present the semblance of youth or old age. The face of the other angel was that of a woman, apparently some ten or fifteen years younger.

The dying woman opened her eyes and into them there came that look of glad recognition I have so often observed in those whose spirits are about to be released forever from their earthly tenements. She stretched forth her two hands. One angel grasped one hand and the other angel the other hand, while their radiant faces were aglow with the joy of welcoming to the better world her whose earthly pilgrimage was finished.

"Oh, Willie," she exclaimed, "you have come to take me home at last, and I am glad, for my sufferings have been hard to bear and I am very tired."

Then she added, "And you, too, Martha!"

With the joyous light still in her eyes, her hands remained outstretched for perhaps half a minute. Then they seemed to slip from the grasp of the angels. All her sufferings were over.

The daughter had raised her head at the sound of her

mother's voice, and her tear-dimmed eyes seemed to reflect something of the glad surprise depicted on her mother's face.

"I can doubt no more after this," she said to me when her mother had breathed her last breath. "I know that mother saw father and her sister, Aunt Martha. I know that they came to take her to her rest in heaven."

Eagerly she listened to me when I told her a little later how I had seen two angels depart with her angel mother.

"I believe it! I believe it!" she cried. "But oh, how I wish that I could have seen it, too!"

I told her that she might some day see her mother in angel form.

"Yes, now I believe that is possible, too," she said.

The thought comforted her greatly and the bitterness of her grief gave way to a feeling of resignation, illumined by a great hope. And that hope was soon realized, for she was one who, unsuspected by herself, possessed unusual psychic powers.

For some two years after her mother's death I saw her at intervals. And she was able to assure me that so far from death having deprived her utterly of her mother's companionship, as she had anticipated when she had abandoned herself to grief, it had brought her a more soul-felt sense of it than she had when her mother was still with her. And added to this was a greater heavenward guidance than her mother had been able to exercise over her when she dwelt in a physical body.

"I still miss her sadly at times," she said to me once, "but

68

whenever I am perplexed by doubts, or worried by troubles, she comes to me and brings me comfort and peace because she turns my thought to God."

Her two brothers, who had been living abroad at the time of their mother's death, returned home soon afterwards. They, too, developed psychic powers similar to those with which their sister was blessed, and were able at times to see their mother and converse with her. And in them, too, this was accompanied by a great spiritual uplifting, so marked that their friends commented on it and sought to learn the cause of it.

TWELVE

In the course of my work as a nurse, several persons came under my observation in whom, through angel ministry, the burden of a great affliction was greatly lightened and wretchedness and despair made to give way to peace and hope. Perhaps the most striking of these happy transformations was that wrought in a crippled girl of sixteen who had been born practically without legs. She was one of several children but she alone of them was deformed. Because of her deformity her parents seemed to be ashamed of her and showed her little affection. She was never taken out of the house and, as far as possible, the neighbors were kept in ignorance of her existence.

She never had been taught even to read or write, and had received no religious instruction whatever.

I never should have known her but for a serious illness in the family which led to my being called in and staying in the house for six months. My heart was touched by her pathetic face and big wistful eyes. At first she shrank from me, as she did from all strangers, because the neglect with which she had been treated had led her to believe that her deformity must arouse feelings of aversion in all who beheld her. That, naturally, only increased my pity for her, and I set myself to work to break down the barriers of her sensitiveness and timidity. In that I soon succeeded, for her famished heart was hungry for affection.

When I had won from her some measure of trust and love, I told her something of God's love and the story of the Savior and His work on earth. She listened to me eagerly. Just as a plant that has dwindled and drooped in a parched soil revives and takes on new life when the rain descends upon it, so, it seemed to me, did her soul, that had been so long groping in the darkness of spiritual ignorance, awaken and expand when brought into the sunshine of divine love.

"Tell me more! Tell me more about it!" she would frequently exclaim, her big eyes lit up with joyous expectancy, when I talked to her of the ministry of the angels and told her that she, too, would some day be as one of them.

"And shall I be able to walk like other people?" she asked me.

72

"Yes," I answered, "when you go to their world you will be given a beautiful spirit body, perfect in every way and be freed from all pain and weariness."

"Oh," she cried, "I do wish that I could see the shining angels, too. I wouldn't feel so lonely then!"

I told her that she might see them some day; that she might even be able to hear them, too; but if she did not she would be able to feel that they were about her. She, too, was one who possessed rare latent powers, which, it seemed, needed only the awakening of her spiritual nature to develop and reveal to her the reality of the ministry of angels.

I had not been in the house quite a month when she told me that she had seen the "shining angels" in a dream. For several nights thereafter she dreamed about them and used to look forward to her slumber with delight because of the comfort these dreams brought her. And one morning when I went to her room to inquire how she had slept, she sat up in her bed, her eyes dancing with delight, and clapped her hands.

"What do you think? What do you think?" she exclaimed gleefully, "I have seen one of the shining angels!"

"In a dream?" I asked.

"No, it wasn't a dream; it was real," she answered. "The angel stood by my bed, where you are standing, and talked to me."

"And what did the angel talk to you about?"

"He talked to me about God's love, like you have done, and he made me feel that God really does love me. And he told me

73

that I should be a shining angel, too, some day, and that I should be able to move about just as they do. Oh, I am so happy, because I know that it is all really, really true."

She clapped her hands and I clapped my hands, too, and a prayer of thanksgiving went up from my heart that the companionship of the angels had been granted her, for I knew that they would bring her greater comfort and peace than could any earthly friends.

After that hardly a day went by, as long as I remained with the family, that she did not tell me that she had seen and talked with one of the angels.

I taught her to read and write. She learned rapidly, for she had naturally a quick mind and thirsted for knowledge. She took great delight in reading the Bible, and told me that the angels used to talk to her about what she read there, and explained things to her and made her feel very happy. Both by day and by night she experienced, at times, this beautiful angel ministry. And she often heard, too, she told me, beautiful music, which I doubt not was the same that I heard.

These revelations wrought a great change in her. The depression which had become habitual to her gave way to a quiet joy which had in it something that was contagious, so that her parents, who before had shunned her, grew to like her and to find pleasure in her society. But they were in no sense spiritually-minded people. They could not believe in the ministry of the angels. They were sure that the girl only imagined that she

74

saw them and talked with them. But since it made her happy they concluded that it would be well to let her cultivate the "delusion," as they termed it.

Her father and mother had been talking to me one day about the matter, and expressing the opinion that it was "contrary to common-sense and all nonsense, of course," when something caused us to go together to the girl's room. There I saw a radiant angel bending over her. Because the time was drawing near when I should have to leave her and I wished to fortify her against the scepticism of her own family, and, if possible, shake a bit of her parents' faith in their own blindness and ignorance, I announced that I could see the angel and I described its appearance.

"Oh, I am so glad that you see the shining angel just as I do," exclaimed the daughter, "for now father and mother will know that it isn't just my imagination."

I was very sorry to leave the girl, for she had developed into a sweet and loveable character. She wept when I bade her good-bye, and said that she would miss me very much.

"But you will never again feel so lonely as you used to feel," I said. "You will always have the angels to comfort you."

"Yes, I know that," she replied, brightening. "They have promised me that so long as I live they will never desert me, and that after I die I shall be with them always."

THIRTEEN

The recognition, while the mind is still clear, of the near approach of death causes men and women, I believe, more than does anything else, to disclose their real characters. Then, it seems to me, the soul throws aside all that has served to conceal its true nature, and shows itself as it really is, beautiful or hideous. And to the nurse, more clearly even than to the doctor or the minister, does the soul, under these circumstances, reveal itself. For the visits of the doctor or minister the patient is, in a measure, generally prepared. Then the habits of a lifetime often reassert themselves and the soul hides itself from scrutiny.

77

But this mask cannot be maintained throughout the long hours that the nurse is in attendance on the patient, especially in the night watches, when the one who has heard the dread summons cannot sleep and wrestles with the question, What comes after death?

Then is shown the great difference between those who have found a satisfactory answer to this question and those who have found none. Death, no less than life, long ago taught me the transcendent importance of religion; of a faith which is awake seven days a week and is not assumed only on Sundays as a concession to conventional respectability. That pretended faith, it has been proved to me again and again, affords no support whatever to the soul in the real crises of life.

Mr. F—— was a profoundly religious man of that fine type which finds in religion a source of constant joy and a sure guide in all the perplexities of life. He was much liked by all who knew him. I was called in to nurse him when he was suffering from pneumonia and in a very critical condition. But the first night I was with him I was made aware that he was the recipient of angel ministry, for by his bed, bending over him, I saw an angel whose features were those of a young man. This angel, as I had so often seen the healing angel do at the hospital, placed his right hand on the sufferer's brow. Every night thereafter, and frequently several times in the course of a night, as long as I remained in the house, I saw this angel by F——'s bedside. At times he seemed to exercise a very soothing influence over the patient, calming his restlessness and enabling him to sleep better.

But despite this ministration and all that the two doctors could do for him, he grew steadily worse. He frequently became delirious. In delirium the dominant note of a man's character often asserts itself. It certainly did with F——. In his delirium he often sang, and sang exultingly, snatches of his favorite hymn:

Soldiers of Christ arise,
And gird your armor on.

The pneumonia developed into double pneumonia and the heart became affected. The doctors who were attending him came to the conclusion that the case was hopeless. The specialist who was called in could only confirm their judgment that it was beyond the power of medical skill to save the patient's life.

That evening, after the specialist had pronounced the death sentence, the family were summoned to F——'s room to take what they feared would be their last leave of him. For him death had no terrors. It was the thought only of the sorrow it would cause his beloved wife and children that saddened him. "It will be my gain but their loss," he said.

After they had all left the room and I was alone with him, he held out his hand to me and said: "Nurse, the end seems

79

very near. Pray for me, and then you will remain with me to the end, will you not?"

I promised him that I would and I prayed for him, the words that I used seeming to be put into my mouth. Then he joined me in repeating the Lord's prayer.

Soon after he became delirious and sang verses of his favorite hymn. About four o'clock in the morning he awoke from a brief sleep fully conscious. After swallowing a little nourishment, he said:

"Nurse, have you been out of the room?"

"No, I have not," I answered.

"Have I been out of the room?" he then asked me.

I assured him that he had not left the room.

"Are you quite sure?"

"Yes, I am quite sure," I replied. "I have been here all night and during that time you have not been out of your bed."

"But I have been away," he said, "for I have seen the Savior and He said to me, 'Keep your armor bright, your work here is not finished yet. You will soon be better and you will have plenty of work to do for Me then.' "

Thinking that he might still be a little delirious, I made some soothing remark to him. But he perceived the doubt that was in my mind.

"Surely you believe me, nurse," he said, "when I tell you that I have seen the Savior? And," he added confidently, "I know now that I shall recover."

80

A little later I saw the bright angel with uplifted hand standing at the head of the bed. In the course of the next few hours there occurred an improvement in his condition, very slight, but to me, who had been watching him so closely, clearly perceptible. I felt that the crisis was past.

The members of the family had been forbidden by the doctors to talk to F——, but I told them what he had told me of seeing the Savior and the assurance he had received that he would recover. They were amazed and awed, but they believed it and the depression that had possessed them gave way to hope. The atmosphere of the whole household was changed from that time. It was as though some holy influence pervaded it which brought with it peace and serenity.

The doctors could find nothing in the very slight improvement in the patient's condition that would justify them in reversing their opinion that he could not possibly recover. I dared not tell them there were agencies at work on his behalf of which *materia medica* took no cognizance. They would have scoffed at the idea.

He continued to improve slowly and at the end of two weeks the doctors pronounced him out of danger. They regarded his recovery as simply marvellous. And, generous as are always members of the medical profession to give credit where they think it is due, they told me they believed it was only my devoted nursing that had saved him. But I knew it was not to me that he owed his recovery.

Of the many deaths I have witnessed that of Mrs. L——
afforded the most striking and beautiful example of the triumph of faith over the "grim terror." It is one of the most
precious of the memories that remain to me of my experiences
as a nurse. Mrs. L—— had been a noted professional singer, to
whose gift of song charities never appealed in vain. She was a
good woman and a most lovable one. She was afflicted with an
internal disease which had been pronounced incurable. I had
seen the dark form with the veiled face at the foot of the bed
and knew that the end was near.

For twenty-four hours she had been so weak and exhausted
that she could scarcely speak above a whisper, and was quite
incapable of raising herself in her bed. Two angels became
visible to me, standing on either side of the bed, and I knew
they had come to conduct her glorified spirit, whose new tenement would soon take shape above the outworn physical body,
to the sphere where peace and joy abide and suffering is unknown.

Suddenly she opened wide her beautiful eyes. She gave no
indication of having recognized the angels, but raising herself
in her bed, her face illumined by a joy that was not of this
earth, she sang, from beginning to end, that magnificent anthem, "O, rest in the Lord!" Her voice rang out as clear and
strong as when in concert halls, in years gone by, hundreds had
listened to it enraptured.

There are some spectacles on earth, it is good to know, which gladden the angels. And this was one of them. For the radiant faces of those two by the bed glowed with a holy delight as they watched and listened to the singer, who was soon to join the heavenly host.

When the song was finished she dropped back in the bed and expired. Then I witnessed her birth into the deathless life, and, as an angel, her departure accompanied by the other two angels, to where rest in the Lord is found always.

Far different was the death of Mrs. T——. She was a wealthy woman, had been a beautiful one, and intellectually was highly gifted. But she was inordinately vain, exceedingly selfish and utterly worldly. Outwardly, because it helped her to gratify her craving for social distinction, she posed as a religious woman. She carried her ostentatious piety so far as to insist that all her servants should attend divine worship at church—no chapel would suffice—once at least every Sunday. It was one of the conditions of their employment.

She, too, was the victim of an internal complaint. Before I was called in she had had in quick succession two nurses, who had left her because they could not endure her domineering manner and unreasonable exactions. But, somehow, I managed to get along with her, and remained with her until her death, which occurred six months after I had been engaged to nurse her.

For two weeks before the end came she knew that her case was hopeless, and that death would soon claim her. Then it was shown me that her assumption of religious fervor and piety had been a mere pretence. When I tried to turn her thoughts to the other life, I discovered that she was as utterly sceptical concerning the reality of a future state of existence as the grossest materialist.

"Nobody knows that there is any life after death," she said. "What religion teaches about the future state is all mere guess work and imagination. We know only that death ends this life."

That others should die had seemed to her natural and had called forth no protest from her, but that death should come nigh her filled her with indignation. Why should she be required to yield up her life, and be deprived of everything that ministered to her comfort and enjoyment?

For her the God whom she had worshipped apparently so devoutly in church did not exist. In the efficacy of prayer, though she had prayed much in public, she had no faith. She found no solace except in railing against the cruelty and injustice of the decree by which her life was to be taken from her. Thinking only of self as long as she retained consciousness, with no ray of hope illumining the darkness that enshrouded her soul, her last days were pitiable to witness.

FOURTEEN

There came a time when I was compelled to give up nursing, and troubles of various kinds weighed heavily upon me. It was the dark hour that preceded the dawn, but I did not know that the dawn was near.

I accompanied a friend to the house of a lady who had been an invalid for many years and needed a nurse. When I met her my heart went out to her at once, for in a moment there was revealed to me the depths and tenderness of her saintly soul. How, I know not; I cannot explain it. This woman, I said to myself, is the friend I have long been seeking, and a great hope came to me that I might win her friendship. But it was for only a brief space that I could entertain it. For while I conversed with her as she lay on a couch, the dark form with the veiled face appeared at the foot of it. I knew then that she would soon die.

My friend was engaged as her nurse, but I wished devoutly that circumstances had permitted me to take the position. I left the house saddened, for it seemed to me that a bitter disappointment had been added to my burdens.

Two days later, at the very time that it occurred, as I subsequently learned, I witnessed her death, though I was not present in my corporeal form. It seemed to me that I was suddenly transported to her room. I heard her utter her last words, "God is love." I saw above her discarded earthly body her glorified spirit form, the radiant face illumined by that wondrous and holy joy which is never seen on the faces of earth's children. And I saw the two angels who had been waiting to depart with her. Then I came to myself, reclining on my own bed in my own room, and wept for the loss of a friend whose friendship I had never known. Little did I realize then what a friend she was to prove to me, what comfort she was to bring to me, and what she was to reveal to me of the life that lies beyond the grave.

One day, within a week after she had gone whither I longed to go, I was alone in my room, kneeling by my bed, praying for help and guidance. I was in sore trouble which involved others who were dear to me and I could discern no way out of it.

86

Something touched me softly on the shoulder, and turning my head I saw her standing by my side, as I had seen her in my vision after she had undergone the wondrous transformation wrought by death.

"Cast thy burdens upon the Lord and He will sustain thee," she said, and slowly vanished from my sight. There are few, if any, texts in Scripture that have afforded greater comfort to those in trouble, but when spoken by an angel the divine message sinks deeper far than when uttered by human lips. I rose from my knees feeling that I had indeed received an answer to my prayer.

But the way out of my difficulties was not immediately disclosed to me. Two days later I was attending to my household duties, but with my mind full of worries, when again I felt a gentle touch on my shoulder, and again I beheld this angel standing by my side. She recited another text: "Fear not, neither be dismayed; I will be with thee; I will not fail thee nor forsake thee."

There was that depicted on her radiant face as she repeated these words which, of itself, conveyed an assurance that God never fails those who trust in Him, and peace came to me.

But human nature is weak and I am very human. It is hard to remain firm in that deep trust in God which affords a calm refuge in all the trials of life while still sore beset. At times I could not help giving way to despondency, and several times in the course of the next week did this angel appear to me, each time reciting some text applicable to my mood and condition. And I was much helped and uplifted thereby.

Before she appeared to me I had, as has been related, seen many angels and some beautiful phases of their ministry had been revealed to me. But I had regarded them as so transformed by death, so exalted spiritually, that they could not come into intimate contact with our earthly lives, circumscribed as we are by limitations to which they are not subject, and harassed by cares and trials from which they have been released. But from her I learned that angels still possess, in a purer form and freed from all earthly alloys, those human feelings, sympathies and affections, which had endeared them to their friends here.

For in the course of time, and a very little time, she became more intimately my friend than any friend I had known who belonged to this life. When she appeared to me it was not to vanish almost immediately, but to stay with me and converse with me as freely and naturally as could any human being. When she was with me I could see her as plainly as I can see any of the everyday objects of life; and her voice, soft, low, melodious, was as distinctly audible to me as is any form of human speech. And she disclosed to me an individuality just as pronounced as that of any person possessed of strong characteristics who still dwells on this earth.

While conversing with her it was not necessary for me to express my thoughts in speech. If I did speak to her she heard me and replied to me; but if I did not speak she read my

88

thoughts equally well and responded to them. With us on earth speech is often used to conceal thoughts. They cannot thus be concealed from an angel friend. And therefore such friendship involves a much closer intimacy than is usual among human friends. Also it imposes higher obligations and fidelity to truth. Apart from the uplifting influence which such a one exercises, the knowledge that the angel reads what is passing in one's mind prevents the harboring of thoughts that are mean and base.

Though we may give no audible expression to them, our thoughts do indeed travel far. When in trouble or distress I had only to wish that she were present to comfort me to find her by my side. Nay, it was not even necessary to wish for her to bring her to me. One does not like to call too often on friends for help. But she could tell when I needed her even though I had not thought of summoning her, and would respond immediately to my need.

She said to me once in these earthly days of our companionship: "Don't think of me as an angel, exalted far above everything that pertains to your everyday life; think of me as your friend who wishes to help you in every way and is interested in everything that concerns your welfare."

She accompanied me often on my walks and talked to me freely about what we chanced to see. She was often with me as I went about my household duties, frequently helping me by suggestions, and by her gaiety and good humor making the tasks seem light and trivial. Though a great sufferer on earth for many years, she had always preserved, as I learned from those who had known her, the bright, sunny, hopeful, helpful spirit that had attracted so many to her before she was smitten with her long illness. And now that she was freed from all weakness and pain she fairly radiated joy and bubbled over with happiness. Her merry, rippling laughter was in itself a tonic. I have written of her in the past tense, but I should have used the present tense. For she is still my dearest friend, and until my earthly pilgrimage is finished, she will continue to counsel, guide and comfort me. She is my guardian angel.

Most of her friends speak of her mournfully as "dead." It is the hope that I may some day be as vitally alive as she is that makes me, at times, long to be numbered among the dead.

FIFTEEN

The path by which I should escape the troubles that beset me had not yet been opened to me. One night I had again fallen into a despondent mood and lay on my bed unable to sleep. I prayed for help. I heard a beloved voice utter my name softly, and my guardian angel, as I was to learn that night she was, was bending over me.

"Come with me," she said, and placing an arm around me she raised me up.

The room vanished from my sight, and with her arm encircling my waist I was wafted—I know no other word that would better describe it—swiftly through space, mounting, it seemed to me, ever higher and higher. We passed over the city, and though it was night and we appeared to be a great height above it, as I looked down I could clearly see the faces of the people in the crowded thoroughfare. I could hear the roar and rattle of the traffic as clearly as though I, myself, were one of the jostling throng. But as we sped onward and upward the sounds gradually became inaudible and the huge city disappeared from my sight. On and on we went, passing over spaces of open country, over towns and rivers and wide stretches of water, always, it appeared to me, rising still higher and higher until earth was lost sight of, and for a brief while I could see nothing.

Then we stopped and I was standing with the angel in the midst of a scene of such wondrous beauty that it filled me with rapture. It did not dawn upon me gradually as we approached it; it burst upon my delighted vision in a moment.

"Where are we?" I asked the angel.

"This is heaven, where we abide," she answered; "and when we come here all cares and troubles are left behind. And now rest."

We sat down together and a great happiness, such as I had never known before, possessed me. All the troubles that had weighed so heavily upon me had indeed been left behind.

I said to the angel: "What a wondrous sense of peace and rest comes over me! Can I stay here always?"

"No; not yet," she replied. "Your work on earth is not yet finished. But you have many friends here and I shall be with you always, for I am your guardian angel."

92

She had not before told me that I was under her special care, and the assurance that her guidance and protection henceforth would always be mine came to me like a precious gift for which I felt grateful beyond words to express.

Then I became aware of a new gift of vision. I could see my own features. But it was not the face that my mirror shows me on earth, but my spirit face that I saw, radiant as were the faces of those glorified beings I had so often seen take shape above their physical bodies from which life had fled, and like them I was clad in a spirit robe. Then I knew that it was in my spirit body I had left the earth where my corporeal body, still alive, remained, and to it I should return to finish my work on earth.

The entrancing beauty of the place to which my guardian angel had brought me is utterly beyond my powers to describe. I can only faintly suggest what it is like. I was in a vast, park-like garden, surrounded by mountains, dimly visible, so far away were they. It compared with the most beautiful of earthly gardens, as the glorified spirit body does with the physical body. There are flowers there in magnificent profusion and trees and shrubs and stretches of greensward, and walks and rivers and streams.

Much of the foliage and many of the blossoms resemble those of earth, but with the wondrous difference I have indicated. Many of the flowers are unlike any I have seen on earth and in loveliness far surpassing them. The same is true of many of the trees and shrubs.

On some of the trees grow fruits that resemble those found

93

on earth; other trees bear fruits that I have never seen here. There are many birds in this Heavenly Garden, but their plumage is far more beautiful, and their notes far more gladsome than are those of any of earth's feathered songsters. The whole place is pervaded by an exquisite and exhilarating fragrance. And the light there is a light that never was on sea or land. The wondrous glow that attends a beautiful sunset when all nature seems to praise God affords a faint conception of what it is like. Great artists seek to idealize the landscapes they paint. But here everything the eye beholds—the light, the colors, the forms—is idealized far beyond the power of any human artist to realize whose vision has been restricted to earthly scenes.

Everywhere were the angel forms of transfigured men and women, both young and old, but all equally buoyant and vigorous, differing in features as do earth's inhabitants, but each countenance radiant with a joy that is unknown in this world, and which invests the plainest face with a charm far transcending that of mere physical beauty.

What a contrast their bright faces were to the many care-oppressed and troubled faces that I had seen in London's crowded streets when I passed over them with my guardian angel! But it was comforting to know that many of those weary and toil-worn men and women who are fighting life's battle bravely would some day be as those I beheld about me.

These angels, it seemed to me, comported themselves much as do happy, kindly people on earth, sitting or walking about,

94

singly or in pairs or groups, pausing now and again to exchange greetings or to converse with friends. There was nothing about them to awaken that feeling of awed surprise which, if some conceptions of the nature of the life that follows this were true, would be aroused on beholding for the first time those who had been transformed by death beyond all semblance to human beings. Angels they were, but still human—glorified human beings.

On earth, amid scenes of great natural beauty, the presence of a multitude of people often jars on one, and makes one less appreciative of nature's handiwork. But in the Heavenly Garden each one of the thousands of angels seemed to contribute something to the beauty and harmony of the scene and the sense of holy peace and joy that possesses one on beholding it.

But oh, the music! How it swelled and pealed, echoed and re-echoed, and then died away in soft, sweet harmonies! And thousands of voices were blended in the songs of praise. Then did I realize whence came the music that I had often heard on earth, but which none of my friends could hear. But here it was even more beautiful and inspiring.

These outbursts of melody and song seemed spontaneous. No signal that I could discern preceded them. Nor could I discover whence came the music like unto that of some wondrous and mighty organ whose tones some gifted musician might, perhaps, hear faintly in his dreams, but only in his dreams. There was nothing that I could perceive correspond-

95

ing to organized choirs such as are common on earth. All joined in the singing and the harmony was perfect. It seemed as though they simply yielded to a simultaneous and irresistible impulse to give vent to the gratitude and love for the eternal Father, which filled their hearts to overflowing. And oh, the joy and gladness of it! It was the audible expression of that feeling which seizes upon some of us in those rare and holy moments when we seem to be brought near to God, and which here we are so powerless to express.

Some of the songs were familiar to me, though rendered with a joyous exultation and perfection of harmony such as is never heard on earth. I joined in the singing of them, for I could not have kept silent had I wished to do so, under the impulse that possessed all there. Many of the songs were unknown to me, but they were all songs of praise and thanksgiving.

Among the throng of angels I recognized many I had known on earth. Some I had nursed. They greeted me with smiles and kindly words. To them I was as one of themselves—one who had passed through the portals of death to reach heaven.

How long I remained there I have no idea. I had no sense of the flight of time. But when I found myself again in my room I knew that it was no dream that had dissipated my gloomy thoughts.

SIXTEEN

*S*ome *two months* after I had been taken to the Heavenly Garden, as I call it, I was sitting by the open window of my bedroom watching the glorious spectacle of the breaking of the dawn. As the sun appeared there fell upon my soul a deep sense of the power and beneficence of the Creator. Suddenly I became aware that my guardian angel was by my side.

"Come with me," she said, and placed an arm around me. Then, as before, the room vanished and we were speeding swiftly through space. The shifting panorama of earth disappeared from view, and again I stood in the Heavenly Garden. Its wondrous beauties, the glorious music and the glad hymns

97

of praise, filled my innermost being with joy and peace.

"Stay here," said my companion, "and I will bring some friends to see you whom you will be very glad to meet."

She disappeared, but in a few moments she was back again. And with her were my father and my mother.

Death causes many sad partings on earth, but it brings also glad meetings in heaven. The grief and sorrow that it brings on earth I had indeed known, and now I experienced the gladness of the meetings that it brings in heaven, but without myself having died. My father I recognized immediately. He was as I had last seen him alive on earth, save that he now stood before me in his glorified spirit form. But, wonderful to relate, although my mother had been taken from me when I was only three years old and my recollections of her form and features had grown vague and dim, I recognized her at once, just as I had my father, and with the same thrill of delight. In all the years that had passed since she left me, her memory had been very precious to me, and I always had the feeling that she was watching over me from some far-off place. It dawned upon me instantly that it was not as one whose life had been hidden from her since she went from me that she greeted me, but as one whose life was known to her as none who had been my most intimate friends on earth had known it. And in the same way I realized also that my father was cognizant of the experiences life had brought me since he had parted from me on earth.

After an embrace, which was as real and tender as ever was that between a mother and daughter on earth, who had been long separated, I said: "Oh, mother dear, now that I have found you at last I want never to leave you again. How often have I cried out for you in the years that are gone when my trials and troubles were hard to bear!"

"Now that you have found me," she replied, "we shall never be long parted again. Henceforth your name shall be 'Joy,' for joy you will bring to many sad and hungry hearts on earth."

Soon after this second visit to the Heavenly Garden, my circumstances changed and my burdens were lifted from me. My mother's promise that we should never be long parted again has been abundantly fulfilled. The day after our meeting in the Heavenly Garden she appeared to me on earth, accompanied by my guardian angel. She was just as plainly visible to me, and able to converse with me as freely. Few days have passed since that first meeting between us where all is joy, peace and harmony that I have not seen her and talked with her. From her I have received the strongest proof that those who loved us so fondly before death took them from us continue to love us still, however long we may be separated from them. The ties of pure affection are strengthened, not weakened by death. A mother when she becomes an angel is a mother still, with all that was best in her nature when on earth refined and intensified.

After that second visit to the Heavenly Garden, my father came to me often, and my brother, too. Old friends, some of

99

whom died long ago, are now numbered among my angel visitors. Among them, too, are some whom I had not known when they lived here, but who have become very dear to me. For, just as a friend on earth brings us in contact with his or her friends, who may also become our friends, so does an angel friend.

Many times since my mother bestowed the name of "Joy" upon me, I have found refreshment for my soul amid the beauties and harmonies of that abode of the angels where none of the jarring discords of the earth ever penetrate. When transported there it has been generally at night, after I have fallen asleep. To other places have I been taken in my spirit body while my physical body lay dormant here, and visions strange and wonderful have been shown me.

Blessed, indeed, am I! Why, I often asked myself in the days when I first became familiar with the beauties of the Heavenly Garden and the delights of angel companionship there, have such glorious privileges been bestowed on me? I had done nothing to merit them. Those psychic powers which have enabled me to penetrate so far beyond this earth life have not been developed by any of those flesh-mortifying and self-denying practices by which I have heard, some devotees of occultism acquire the power to vacate their physical bodies at will. But I had not long pondered over this question before the answer to it was given me by my guardian angel.

"Much has been revealed to you of the ministry of the angels on earth, and you have been freely admitted to their abode in heaven," she said, "that you may tell the world something of what you have learned. For on earth there are many sore perplexed and troubled who, through angel ministry, did they know how to avail themselves of it, could obtain such aid, solace and light, that their despondency would give way to joy and their scepticism be replaced by certain knowledge that God is indeed love. Then will they know what it is to have the kingdom of heaven within."

The solace and uplifting that this blessed experience brings, I learned from my guardian angel, had been granted her in her earth life, especially in the long years that she had been an invalid. She, too, had been able to see angels and converse with them.

The idea of writing a book about what had been revealed to me filled me with dismay. My work as a nurse had left me little leisure even for the reading of books, in which I found great delight, and my writing had been restricted to occasional hastily scribbled letters; but it was pointed out to me that I had already been brought into close association with one who would help me to accomplish the task for which I felt unfitted.

SEVENTEEN

*M*any *blended voices* sounded in my ears and a great volume of song that seemed to burst spontaneously from thousands of glad hearts filled to over-flowing with divine love. "Glory to God in the highest!" they sang until the echoes died away in melodious whispers among the trees. I was again in the Heavenly Garden with my guardian angel, whose face seemed then to take on a new radiance and beauty.

"It is good to be here, Joy," she said. "And now come with me."

She led me to what I must liken to a broad thoroughfare or street, which extended until lost in the far distance. It was covered with turf soft and springy, and of that lovely green hue that is seen in favored climes in springtime, but more beautiful. On either side, standing side by side, were what would correspond to houses on earth. They were all, it appeared to me, of uniform size and height and of marble whiteness. Each of them had a single lofty entrance, but nothing I could discern that corresponded to windows.

My guardian angel led me through one of the entrances and I found myself in a spacious chamber filled with a subdued light, and in which various shades of color were blended in such perfect harmony that it impressed one as some beautiful and soothing music made visible. The walls were hung with cloud-like draperies, in which greens, pinks, crimson and golds were blended so artistically that there was nowhere a jarring note of color. But the draperies were unlike any of the earth's textile fabrics. They were distinctly visible to me, but they offered no resistance to my touch. It was like thrusting my hand into a cloud. In the chamber there were several couches that displayed the same soothing, harmonious coloring. Many plants and beautiful flowers were bestowed about the place.

"This," said my guardian angel, "is my rest chamber where I come to rest and meditate. And you shall come here and rest with me, often."

We sat on one of the couches and talked.

"Who builds these beautiful rest chambers?" I asked.

"It is the will of the Supreme that builds them," she answered. "We find them prepared for us and awaiting us when we come here. Each of the angels here is provided with a rest chamber similar to this."

"Dear," I said, "I used to think that when a redeemed spirit left its earthly abode, it ascended direct to a state of perfect bliss and there remained with God throughout eternity. Is it not so?"

"No," she answered, "none attain to perfection immediately after death. Many here passed through other spheres, after leaving earth, before they attained this one. The unending life that follows death is, for those who seek good and not evil, a life of progression. You are told, you know, 'In my Father's house are many mansions.' There are worlds and states of existence far higher than this. But here we find happiness in serving God such as is only dreamed of on earth, for here we realize, as we could not there, what God's love is."

On some of my subsequent visits to this rest chamber my mother accompanied me there. And sometimes she has taken me to her own rest chamber. There the color scheme is somewhat different, crimson and pale blue being the predominant shades, but their effect on me was equally soothing and restful. The colors in these rest chambers, I have been told by one the angels, reflect the spiritual qualities of the occupants, and as these differ among the angels, so do the predominant hues of the rest chambers.

I had been often to the Heavenly Gardens before it fully dawned upon me what it is that imparts to it its heavenly quality. It is not its sublime beauty, nor its glorious music, nor its wondrous light, nor its fragrance, nor the radiant forms and faces of the angels who abide there. It is not any one of these things, nor all of them combined, which makes it heavenly. It is the deep, continuous sense of the love of God which fills all hearts there.

As I could tell by the varying types of features, the angels there belonged, when on earth, to various nations and races, whose religions—the form in which they were expressed at least—may have differed widely, but in the state in which they now live this deeply felt knowledge of God's love and the reciprocal feeling it awakens in their breasts, they all have in common, and by it are united in the ties of brotherhood.

Many of them, I learned, are still keenly interested in what takes place on earth, especially in the discoveries, inventions and social movements by which civilization progresses. I have sometimes listened to a group of such discussing, perhaps, the latest developments in the application of electricity to industry and the wonders still to be accomplished by it; or flying machines and what remains to be done before aerial navigation is rendered safe and of commercial utility.

In the midst of such converse there might be heard one of those glorious bursts of music which, ever and anon, resound in the Heavenly Garden, and with one accord they would join in singing the song of praise and thanksgiving, not perfunctorily, as is often done in religious gatherings on earth, but gladly and whole-heartedly.

106

One whom I had heard take part in several of these discussions and who, on earth, had been a clever engineer and scientist, said to me: "God's love is to us here as is the air they breathe to those who live on earth. Without it existence here would have little meaning for us, and we should long to return to earth to engage afresh in its struggles and distractions. I am still much interested in those things which on earth occupied such a large share of my thoughts, but still more—far more—am I interested now, though I was not then, in all that makes for the spiritual uplifting of mankind. For vastly more depends on that than on what is called material progress."

On one of my many visits I was walking with my guardian angel by the side of a beautiful stream and yielding myself gratefully to the spirit of peace, rest and adoration that pervades the place, when we beheld a host of angels approaching. They were formed in procession, rank on rank, and there were many thousands of them, all singing songs of praise as only angels can sing. As the front ranks drew near I perceived at the head of the procession one who was visibly clad in glory. From his white robe there radiated light and around his head there shone a bright halo.

"Jesu salvator hominum!" exclaimed my guardian angel, and we fell on our knees. As the Savior passed us He smiled upon us and with uplifted hand bestowed a blessing on us. We remained on our knees for a space silent.

EIGHTEEN

*A*s, *in imagination*, we can transport ourselves to different places on earth, and, with the mind's eye, see the scenes there, so can the angels, with equal speed, actually transport themselves to any spot on earth that they may wish to see, or where there may be work for them to do for God. All the wonders and beauties of this world are accessible to them, and they need employ no other means of locomotion than their own volitions to reach them. And though the beauties of the heavenly spheres far transcend those of earth, the wondrous works of the Creator here still possess great attractions for them. Indeed they derive from them, some of the angels have told me, a keener, loftier delight than they could when in their physical bodies on earth: because, as spirits, they are relieved of all the cares and infirmities that oppressed them here; their thoughts are freer and can soar higher. And in the spirit body, as I had discovered, all the senses are quickened. Colors appear more vivid. As seen by the eyes of the spirit body, earth's beauties are far more beautiful than when seen by the physical eyes. Truly here we see "as through a glass, darkly."

I was once talking with my guardian angel about the difference between earth's scenery and that of the Heavenly Garden.

"There is no sea here," I remarked, "and I suppose that is in fulfilment of the promise that there shall be no more sea."

"There is no sea here, it is true," she said, "but we can go and look at the ocean in any of its moods whenever we wish to do so. Come with me and I will show you."

She placed an arm around me and I was conscious of passing through space at what seemed to me tremendous speed. A few moments only had elapsed, it appeared to me, when I found myself standing by her side on the summit of a very high cliff and looking down on a vast expanse of sea on which there were many ships. In the brilliant sunshine it was a glorious spectacle.

After my first visit there I was taken several times to the summit of this cliff, and once when a fierce storm was raging and great waves thundered against the rocks far below us.

What impressed me greatly, as indicating the difference in

susceptibility to sensations between our spirit bodies and our physical bodies, was the fact that, though I was keenly sensible to all that was exhilarating and uplifting in the scene; though I could smell the salt sea air and inhale it with delight; though I could feel the rush of the wind on my cheeks and exult in it, I experienced none of the discomforts that I should have felt had I been there in my physical body. When the storm was raging fiercely I was not conscious of making any effort to prevent myself being swept off my feet by the wind. On a very cold day I was unconscious of the cold. Changes in temperature are not felt by the spirit body.

I have been taken in my spirit body to India, to South Africa and to other places, near and distant, on earth; but always, it has seemed to me, the time occupied on the journeys was only a few moments. But when in the spirit body I lose all consciousness of the flight of time which, on earth, except when much preoccupied or very happy, we always realize to some extent. Angels have told me that time does not exist for them as it does for earth's inhabitants.

In the Heavenly Garden my conversations with my guardian angel often turned upon my experiences during the day and their lessons. It was natural, therefore, that after having seen some distressing cases of poverty I should speak to her about the hardships of the poor, and of the cruel oppression to which they are often subjected by hard, grinding task-masters.

"There is much more of that oppression on earth than you

are aware of," she said. "Many misguided men are rendered absolutely merciless by their greed for gold, and even little children, thousands of them, are among the victims of their avarice. Come with me and I will show you.'

The scene changed. We were in a big city. We stood before a huge, barrack-like building which she said was a canning factory. I saw many men who were seeking work turned away from the entrance gate, while a lot of women and children were admitted. Some of the latter were hardly more than babes.

We entered the factory and went through it. And there we saw scores of little children toiling hard. Many of them were poorly nourished and scantily clad. They showed none of that joy in life which is the natural heritage of childhood. As they bent over their tasks, their tiny fingers worked nimbly, many sighs went up from them, and some of them were crying bitterly.

"Cannot something be done," I said, "to prevent greedy, hard-hearted men making little children work like this?"

"Joy," she answered, "the men who do it are ignorant men— spiritually ignorant—which is the worst kind of ignorance. Truly, they know not what they are doing. Could they but realize what shackles they are forging for their own souls and what they are preparing for themselves hereafter, could they but see themselves now as we see them, and as they will see themselves after death claims them, they would sooner work their own fingers to the bone and endure the direst poverty

112

themselves than make these little children slave as they do.

"But, Joy," she added, "the day is coming when such men, and many others, will have their spiritual sight opened and the angels will be able to instruct them. Then their hearts will be changed, and they will take delight in doing what they can to make little children happy, for of such is the kingdom of heaven."

I have said that we went through the factory. That is a literal statement of fact. We passed through walls and partitions as we went from one department to another of the huge building. Neither brick walls nor steel beams offered the slightest resistance to our progress.

When I saw angels on earth, in the days before I had learned by my own experience the great difference between the spirit body and the physical body, I used often to wonder how they entered houses and rooms in which no doors were open, and how they left them when all exits were closed.

What to us on earth are solid walls, appear, when approached close by one in the spirit body, as though composed of something like fog. And to the passage of the spirit body through them, they present just as little impediment as does fog to the passage of the physical body. To the spirit vision they are not opaque. In my visits in the spirit body to places on earth, the angel with me has sometimes told me to look into some building; and I have found that to my sight, the building, of whatever composed, was practically transparent. I could see

THE MINISTRY OF ANGELS

through the walls and all that was within was visible to me.

Explain it, I cannot. I can only state it as a fact. Many things that are insoluble mysteries to the human understanding appear just as little mysterious to the spirit faculties, when the spirit is freed from the physical body, as seem to us here the common things and experiences of everyday life. To find one's progress here stopped by a brick wall occasions no surprise. And, similarly, it occasions no surprise to one in the spirit body, to find that the brick wall presents no impediment.

NINETEEN

*A*gain I was watching the beautiful dawn of another day. I saw the sun rise, flooding the eastern sky with roseate light. To me it seemed to bring from on high, as this glorious spectacle always does, a proclamation of God's love for mankind. I fell to thinking of the vast multitude who know nothing of this wondrous love, whose lives are lived in spiritual darkness, who suffer much and know not where to turn for support and comfort. I was filled with pity for them, and a cry went up from my heart that I might be given the wisdom and strength to do something that would help them.

Then my mother came to me and embraced me. "Come

with me," she said, and took me by the hand and together we ascended to the Heavenly Garden.

"Now, behold!" she said, pointing downwards.

I was gazing down on a huge city. I was conscious of being a great height above it and yet I could see the people who thronged its streets as plainly as though I had been close to them, and the noise of the traffic sounded loud in my ears.

Most of the people had that stamped on their faces which showed that the souls within them were famished, but mingling freely with them was a host of angels. By the side of nearly everyone in the crowded thoroughfare was one of these radiant figures.

"Who are these bright ones?" I asked my mother. "And what are they doing?"

"They are some of those," she replied, "who, when they lived on earth, were sorely tried in divers ways, as are many of those by whose side they walk. But they fought life's battles bravely and conquered. And thereby they gained the knowledge, experience and wisdom which fits them to be ministering angels to those who are passing through trials and temptations similar to the trials and temptations which beset themselves in their earthly careers."

"How do they minister to them, mother?" I asked.

"By striving to impress them with thoughts of patience, of courage, of God. By seeking to implant ideas in their minds that will give them nobler aspirations than that of living mainly to gratify their animal natures or selfish ambitions. Often, very often, they fail, for often, alas, the minds of those they strive to influence are too darkened by gloomy, selfish, or debasing thoughts to admit the light the angels would bring them.

"But the angels watch and wait for some opening in the mental clouds which befog such minds, through which they may be able to send some uplifting thought. Perhaps the emotion aroused by witnessing some generous or heroic deed, by reading some inspiring passage in a good book, or listening to some strains of music, may provide the opportunity they seek.

"And often they succeed in turning erring footsteps in the right direction; often they are able to implant in human minds some seed thoughts that germinate and bear fruit that gives a nobler impetus to their lives. Little do men and women realize whence often come those inspiring thoughts which give them renewed hope and courage to take up life's burdens afresh.

"If people could only be made to realize that there are angels watching over them, ever eager and anxious to help them to resist temptation, to conquer selfishness, to develop their spiritual natures, to seek abiding peace where it can alone be found, they would avail themselves of this God-sent help. Then humanity would not long present the sad spectacle it now does to us."

"I can see, mother," I said, "that such knowledge would indeed prove a great blessing to mankind."

"Yes, my child, the greatest of blessings it would be. A prayer went up from your heart this morning that you might be shown how to do something that would help earth's ignorant and suffering children. This vision has been given to you because of that prayer. And that has been revealed to you which will enable you to give the world the message that it sorely needs."

The vision faded from my sight. My eyes beheld only the entrancing beauties of the Heavenly Garden; my ears heard only the glad songs of praise from the angel throng.

TWENTY

I was once more in the Heavenly Garden with my mother and again she bade me look down. And again I beheld the big city beneath me. But it was now night there and the crowded streets were lit up by gas and electric lights. In the public-houses the lights blazed brightly, and on them my eyes seemed focussed. I saw many men and women enter them. Mingling with them were bright ministering angels. And mingling with them, too, were spirits whose faces were not radiant and whose robes were dark-hued.

"Who are those dark ones, mother?" I asked.

"They are some of those who, when living on earth, succumbed to its temptations and became debased and depraved," she replied. "And now they still shut out the light of divine love from their souls, and seek to impel others to become what they themselves were on earth. For it is still their delight to work evil."

I watched some of the dark ones. I noticed they were most numerous among the groups that were carousing most freely. And when some in these groups gave way to anger and fell to quarreling, an expression of coarse delight came into the faces of the dark ones, much like that I once saw depicted on the faces of some half-dozen men of low type who were gathered around a couple of dogs that were fighting savagely. When a man staggered forth drunk, one or more of these dark forms went out with him. And many of them stood about the doors and one or more entered with most of the men and women who passed within.

I observed the work of the bright angels. They seemed to deter several from entering who had hesitated at the doors. I saw one of them lay a hand on the shoulder of a man who had just drained a glass at the counter, and the man seemed to be suddenly reminded of something and left the place. And I saw another lay a hand on a man who had just been uttering angry words, and he, too, seemed suddenly to be reminded of something, and withdrew from the group of quarreling men. But often, I noted, the bright ones made no impression on those they were trying to help, and then they looked saddened.

My father was amongst those who were engaged in this rescue work. I saw him lead forth, one by one, a dozen men and set them on their homeward way, accompanying each of them a little distance before returning to the scene of his labors. I felt very proud of him then, quite as much as I did in earlier years before he was taken from me, when some friend of his had told me of some deed of valor he had performed in the Indian Mutiny.

When the vision had vanished, my guardian angel and my mother talked with me about what had been shown me. They told me that the belief, held by many on earth, that those who after death became angels entered a sphere where they ceased from all labor and passed their lives in praising God and blissful repose, was erroneous. Everyone of the angels, they said, worked and found joy in the work, for it was work for God.

"How could we be happy here," said my mother, "knowing that there is so much misery and spiritual ignorance on earth, if, having the power to help the sinning, benighted and suffering, we did not exercise that power? Some of us work not alone on earth for the uplifting of humanity, but also in the lower spheres to help those spirits who, when on earth, failed to learn life's lessons aright. There are many angels doing what on earth would be called missionary work among those evil spirits, who, as you have seen, seek to lure men and women to destruction."

"It is in the work we are able to do after death," said my guardian angel, "that many of us find rich compensation for the burdens laid on us on earth which ofttimes were so hard to bear. For we realize here that it is often the lessons we learned on earth that were hardest to learn, which best fit us to help some of those now on earth who are being similarly tried.

"On earth, as you know, I was for many years a great invalid. It was that experience which has given me the knowledge and the power to minister to many of those who lie on beds of sickness, oppressed by pain and weariness. I go to the bedsides of many such, and to some I am able to impart thoughts from which they obtain patience, courage, hope, and faith in God. At such times I am glad that I was a great sufferer on earth."

To every human being, they told me, is assigned a guardian angel, whose special duty it is to watch over that person and to strive to help him or her to resist temptation and lead a good life—the life that meets with such blessed reward.

"But how comes it?" I asked my guardian angel, "that an angel can watch so devotedly over one, as you do over me, and yet minister also to others?"

"Because, Joy," she answered, "it is not necessary for guardian angels to be always with those of whom they have charge in order to know what they are doing, or of what they are thinking. Wherever I am, in the Heavenly Garden as you call it, or somewhere on earth far distant from where you live, your thoughts reach me, and if they imply a need of my help, like a flash of light I am by your side."

"Does it sadden the angels to see those they love on earth in trouble and distressed?" I asked.

122

"It does at times," said my mother, "but not to the extent it would if we were like earth's inhabitants. For we here see, as those still on earth cannot see, how often conflict with trials and difficulties strengthens character, develops spirituality, and brings out the best that is in a man or woman. Our vision extends beyond the grave, and we can see what awaits many here, who, to earthly eyes, are overwhelmed by misfortune. Many on earth who are accounted wretched failures by those who know them—or think they know them, are regarded by us among the noblest types of success, because, though poor in worldly goods, they have enriched their souls with those things that are imperishable. And many who on earth are regarded as brilliantly successful are known by us to be wretched failures, because, however great their possessions, they are seen by us to have poverty-stricken souls.

"To our visions, the garments, and the forms of earth's children whom they clothe, are not opaque as they are to those who see only with physical eyes. The true spiritual natures are discerned by us. Human beings are imperishable spirits, just as much as we are, and as such we see them. They should try to realize what they really are, and not think of themselves as beings whose lives cease at death. Then the thoughts of many would be less centered on material things; they would appraise them at their true value, and they would perceive that poverty and riches, in the truest sense, are of the spirit."

I did not at the time comprehend the depth of meaning in that phrase. "Poverty and riches are of the spirit," and how widely it applies to this life of ours here. Subsequently an angel, to whom I am much indebted for much instruction, made it clear to me. He did so by telling me this story.

"A young man took counsel with himself as to what be should make of himself, and resolved that he would become a very rich man, for it seemed to him that with abundant wealth he could obtain all the things that make life worth living.

"To acquiring a large fortune he devoted himself with great energy and singleness of purpose, and he realized his ambition; for mentally he had been generously endowed and blessed with a constitution that could withstand the strain of incessant work.

"When he was nearing threescore he retired from business, intending to enjoy to the full the things that his money could purchase for him. He bought a large estate in the country and built upon it a magnificent house. He called to his aid clever men and skilled craftsmen, and they made of his house a temple of art and of his broad acres a feast of sylvan and horticultural beauty.

"He threw his estate open to the public on certain days. Among those I saw there one day was a man who, judged by the standard of the world, had made a failure of his life, for at fifty-five he still had to work hard for a small salary, and he had very little money laid by. When he entered the grounds and saw how lovely they were, he breathed a prayer of thanksgiving to his Heavenly Father, for he had a soul attuned to beauty, which was to him one of the many proofs of the beneficence of the Creator.

124

"He knew it not, but there were angels with him, for his was a nature keenly receptive to their ministry, and they impressed upon him holy and uplifting thoughts, and interpreted to him the messages of the birds, the trees, the flowers, the brooks and the glades, so that they all spoke to him of the love of God. Peace came to him and joy, and he passed several happy hours wandering over the beautiful estate. He felt rich that day.

"While he was revelling in the feast of beauty, and finding refreshment for his soul, I observed the man who owned the estate. He was pacing his library moodily, a prey to discontent and dejection, for his possessions had not brought him the happiness which he had expected to derive from them when he spent his money so lavishly upon them. It had dawned upon him that though he could buy nearly every material thing that people covet, he could not buy happiness. He was troubled, because, as everybody does, he craved happiness. And he could not discover how he could get it.

"The pursuit of wealth had brought into play only one side of his nature. The other side—the spiritual side—whose cultivation would have yielded such precious fruit, had been undeveloped. He had become, and prided himself on it—an intensely practical man. He believed only in the things of which his five senses could testify. The flowers, the trees, the birds—all the beautiful things he had gathered about him—had no message for his soul. Their spiritual meaning escaped him.

125

"When the dark mood was upon him, no prayer came from his heart for help and guidance. God was for him but a great Perhaps. That passage of Scripture, so often proved profoundly true, 'In all thy ways acknowledge Him and He will direct thy paths,' told him nothing. The angels who fain would have ministered to him could not do so, because those avenues by which their thoughts might have reached his soul he had closed to them. He was not a bad man. Wise only in his own conceit, he was, though he little suspected it, a very ignorant man.

"Now the other man—the man who had failed—had cultivated his spiritual nature. Troubles and sorrows many he had known, but they had made him turn to God for solace and comfort. Thereby he had grown rich in spirit. In the deepest sense, it was not the rich man who had the title deeds to the property in his safe, who owned the beautiful estate. Its beauties belonged to the poor man. It was he who that day realized the fulfillment of the promise. 'Seek ye first the Kingdom of God and His righteousness, and all these things shall be added unto you.' "

TWENTY-ONE

It is, I believe, the experience of most people of earnest and aspiring natures that at times they do realize in a measure the deepest longings of their souls. The doubts and perplexities with which they have long battled vanish; their troubles no longer weigh upon them, and something of that peace which passeth understanding comes to them. They discover that without struggle, without conscious effort, they have obtained that for which they have so ardently yearned. In the spiritual atmosphere to which they then seem transported, all the jarring discords of earth are stilled and a deep content possesses them. They can cherish no grievances then; they are incapable of envy; they can feel no resentment even against those who have wronged them most.

At such times even those who ordinarily are accounted commonplace men or women are transformed and exalted, and radiate a benign influence on all about them. In such moods they feel they have but to listen to the voiceless messages from some source without themselves to find rich refreshment for their souls.

It is then that the angels of God minister to those who have hungered and thirsted after righteousness and give them foretastes of heaven. Such blessed moments might be far more frequent and enduring did those who are seeking spiritual enlightenment recognize this and learn how to obtain the help of the angels.

With those who abide in what I have called the Heavenly Garden, this serene joyousness, in a much larger measure, is ever with them. It is the permanent attainment of this state of mind, realized here only in a lower form, and that rarely, which impressed me as constituting the most striking change that had taken place in those I had known on earth whom I met as angels. I wish I had the power to describe it, so that others might comprehend it, the wonderful charm, the tenderness, the helpfulness, the spiritual power, possessed by all of those, however much their lots may have differed in this life, who have undergone this blessed transformation. If, for instance, I could depict N——, of whose sore trials I have told something in these pages, as he now is, and as I have seen him, it would, I am sure, give renewed hope and courage to many heavily burdened and despondent ones who are struggling, as he had to struggle on earth, against bitter poverty and heart-breaking sorrow.

Though such brave souls may here lead lowly and obscure lives, and leave behind them no records of noble deeds by which large numbers are stirred to emulation, in heaven they are numbered among life's heroes.

When nursing among the dwellers in the slums while on the hospital staff, I heard often of a young curate who had chosen as his field of labor the most squalid quarter of the city. The poor people there spoke of him as "the man," with the accent on the "the" to distinguish him from all other men they knew. When I got to know him too, I recognized the appropriateness of the title they had bestowed on him. Many good men have I met since, some of whom have won distinction in the service of the Church, and others in various walks of life, but he still holds the place of *the* man in my memory.

Tall, well-proportioned, athletic, handsome, he would have attracted admiring notice anywhere. But it was the soul of him that made him *the* man. He seemed to rid himself of every vestige of selfishness. Whole-heartedly, joyously, he devoted his spendid gifts, spiritual, moral, intellectual, physical, to the service of the Master among the denizens of the slums. No man was ever freer from anything suggestive of cant. Always his example squared with his precepts. He carried with him an atmosphere which of itself was an incitement to true manliness. Those who had sunk to the lowest depths of debasement could not withhold from him the tribute of respect. Many a human wreck he reconstructed and made a man of. Among the poor he was greatly loved and revered. On any question of right and wrong that might arise among them, the simple statement that *the* man had said this or that concerning it was regarded as settling the point at issue beyond dispute.

I lost track of him within a short time after leaving the hospital. I never heard his name mentioned among those who had attained prominence in the Church. But I often thought how glorious would be the recognition he would receive in heaven. From a friend—a sea captain—who had known *the* man when I had known him, and had himself years ago entered the haven of rest in heaven, I heard of *the* man's reception there which he had witnessed.

The Savior was passing by when two bright angels brought him whose earth life had ceased but a little while before, to the Heavenly Garden. When the Savior came to where they were standing He laid a hand on *the* man's head and said:

"Well done, good and faithful servant! Welcome home!"

And the angel host took up the cry, "Welcome home! Welcome home!"

Thus was answered for *the* man the query that ran through the refrain of his favorite hymn:

130

Will they sing on that beautiful shore,
Welcome home! Welcome home!
A welcome in Heaven for me?

Life's hard battles leave scars and sore wounds that are seldom healed here. But they are there. There is no sadness there in recalling the trials and sorrows that were bravely met here. They are regarded by the angels as experiences that have brought rich rewards, because thereby has been obtained the knowledge and power that enables them to minister to others who are being similarly tried.

If such could only realize that there are about them many angels who bore when on earth what they now bear, and would avail themselves of their help which is so gladly, lovingly offered, then indeed would their loads be lightened, their lives brightened and their souls illumined by the joy of a great and certain hope, and they would strive ever to fight the good fight whatever the odds against them.

Both in the New and the Old Testaments there are many accounts of intercourse between human beings and angels. And in no instance are such occurrences related as though they so far transcended ordinary human experience as to be deemed incredible. On the contrary, they are related as though they were just as natural as any other phase of spiritual or religious experience. Most Christians profess to believe that these Scriptural narratives are statements of fact.

ome hymns are still sung in churches which joyfully proclaim the faith of the assembled worshippers in the reality of angel ministry even in these modern days. I have heard more than one congregation sing with pious fervor:—

They come, God's messengers of love,
They come from realms of peace above,
From homes of never-fading light,
From blissful mansions ever bright.

They come to watch around us here,
To soothe our sorrow, calm our fear:
Ye heavenly guides, speed not away,
God willeth you with us to stay.

But chiefly at its journey's end,
'Tis yours the spirit to befriend,
And whisper to the faithful heart,
"O Christian soul, in peace depart."

And yet, despite the zest with which many Christians join in the singing of this hymn, the great majority of them, I am convinced, do not really believe it. Strange it is that Christians generally are as contemptuously sceptical as are the grossest materialists concerning every experience in these twentieth-century days which may be adduced as proof that life continues after death, and that the so-called dead, as is often recorded in

132

the Bible, may and do communicate with the living. If they really believe these Biblical narratives I cannot understand on what grounds they so stubbornly maintain that such things are impossible at the present time.

There is much more truth than poetry in the verses of the hymn that I have quoted. It will be a glad day for Christendom when those who sing this hymn really believe what they sing, and the churches and other agencies for spreading the glad tidings of the Gospel proclaim their faith in the ministry of the angels and avail themselves of the help of the angels.

TWENTY-TWO

*T*he *spirit* after death, so angels have told me, enters a sphere of existence which corresponds to its own state. This is in accordance with a law to which all spirits are subject, which may be compared to that of gravity on earth as it affects physical objects. The life led here determines whether the spirit rises or falls after it leaves the body. If the life here has been a good one then it goes to a sphere where it finds rest and happiness and stimulus to further progress. If the life here has been an evil one it goes to a sphere where it suffers. Always the spirit reaps what it has sown. As there are spheres adapted to the various stages of its upward progress, so are there others

135

fitted to its retrograde state. Something of two of these latter has been shown me.

In my spirit body I was facing a pathway of light on which stood a bright angel who beckoned to me. I walked along this pathway and came to the edge of a great forest. The light there was like that often seen in London on a dull, misty winter afternoon when the sun is completely hidden by a low-lying, rain-laden, leaden sky, and within doors lights are needed to read by. The aspect of the forest was somber and depressing in the extreme.

Flitting among the trees were the spirit forms of thousands of men and women of various ages. What a contrast they presented to the angels in the Heavenly Garden! There, every face is aglow with a holy peace and joy, but here every face wore an expression of deep unrest, misery and despair. The Heavenly Garden resounds with glad songs of praise, but the only sounds heard in this gloomy forest were the sighs and wailings that went up from the host of wretched spirits.

Their robes were dark-hued, almost black. They all appeared to be irresistibly impelled to seek for something which they could not find. Their actions reminded me somewhat of those of someone on earth who suddenly discovers that he has lost something which he prizes highly and starts hastily searching for it without any idea where it is to be found. They hurried hither and thither among the trees, glancing eagerly about them, anon slackening their pace as though some faint hope

136

that they were near the object of their search had come to them, for they would then cease their wailing, weeping or sighing. But it was always for a few moments only. The hope, if hope it were, vanished almost immediately and they again resumed their unavailing, anxious seeking, and their cries and gestures of despair.

Though occasionally two or three of them would come together, as they chanced for a brief space to pursue the same direction, they never engaged in conversation that I observed. Each individual seemed so absorbed in his own woes that he took no notice of anybody else. Misery is said to love company on earth, but there was no indication that it found any solace in that here.

I watched these spirits for what seemed to me a long time, for I wondered what it was they were all looking for. Then I became aware that one of them had approached me and was standing by my side. I could tell by his features that he was a middle-aged man when death had claimed him on earth, and one, apparently, who had been endowed with excellent mental powers.

"Can you tell me," I said, turning to him, "what it is that those here are all seeking so eagerly and anxiously?"

He looked at me as though greatly surprised to see me there. "How came you here?" he asked.

I told him that I had come by following a pathway of light.

"Oh, bright spirit," he said, "that is what we here are look-

137

ing for—light. Light where we can find again the opportunities we lost on earth for doing useful work, for doing good, for love. But above all else we are seeking, ever seeking, lost peace of mind and rest, but finding them never.

"Oh, help us, bright spirit, for we are in torment. We are striving continuously, but never accomplishing anything. We want to speak to those whom we left on earth, but we cannot reach them. We want to warn them to make the most of their time, talents and opportunities on God's beautiful earth—to do good to others, and not to seek only the gratification of their own selfish desires. We want to exhort them to take advantage of that freedom of choice which is given to man on earth and choose wisely, for that freedom is not found in this world of shades.

"Here all things are elusive. As you reach out to grasp that which you seek and desire, it is withdrawn; and still you must go on seeking and striving but never attaining, on and on without end. Think what that means! Nothing to hope for! If men were deprived of hope on earth they would sink into black despair."

Wringing his hands and moaning, he passed into the forest to continue his seeking for that which he could never find there.

Then I suddenly found myself in the bright sunshine of the outer world again. A great wave of compassion for those unhappy ones I had just seen swept over me. I thought of how the Savior had ministered to the spirits in prison, and I fell on my

138

knees and prayed that I might be shown how to do something to help them.

My guardian angel came to my side and took me by the hand, and together we ascended to the Heavenly Garden. There I told her what I had seen that had made me feel so sad.

"Come with me and rest awhile," she said, and took me to her rest chamber. How different was the atmosphere there from that of the gloomy under-world forest! The rest chamber radiated peace and joy and hope. Despite what I had been told by the poor wretch who had left me, moaning and wringing his hands, I could not believe that the lot of such was forever utterly hopeless.

My guardian angel read my thoughts. "Joy," she said, "to those unhappy victims of their self-created delusions in the underworld there will come a time, though, perhaps, far distant for some of them, when they will obtain another opportunity to work out their own salvation. And they may yet find rest."

TWENTY-THREE

*A*gain, by a pathway of light, I had reached the dim forest of the underworld. But this time I seemed to have penetrated far into it. I stood on the brink of a deep canyon, through which, far below, ran a swift-flowing river, and, from the height at which I looked down upon it, its color was of an inky blackness.

On my first visit to this gloomy region the apparently utterly hopeless condition of the wretched, restless spirits who inhabited it had chilled my soul. But now I was to learn that God had not abandoned them, and that even here His bright angels were permitted to enter and minister to the miserable victims of their own selfishness and mis-used opportunities on earth.

In the forest, on that side of the stream on which I stood, I beheld, as I had before, thousands of dark-hued spirit forms flitting among the trees, seeking that which they could never find there, and filling the air with their lamentations. To my imagination it seemed that the river was a river of tears—of the tears that had been shed through countless ages by the legions of miserable beings who, through the portals of death, had passed from the bright earth to the gloomy forest.

In that portion of the forest on the other side of the stream I saw no spirits flitting among the trees, and from it no sounds of wailing reached my ears. Just opposite where I stood was a bright angel whom I recognized as my brother. Gathered about him were about a score of dark-hued spirits, but they had ceased wailing, and seemed to be no longer seeking what they could not find.

My brother came to me and I asked him who were those spirits with him.

"They are spirits," he replied, "who, by their genuine repentance for their misdeeds on earth, and their sincere desire to warn others against living as they did there, have earned entrance into another sphere, whither I am conducting them. There they can begin to work out their own salvation, and thus, if they persevere, progress from sphere to sphere until they, too, become ministering angels as are those in heaven."

I told him what the spirit who spoke to me when I first entered the forest had said to me.

"Perhaps, ere now, he has been led to that sphere to which I am taking those whom I have rescued," said my brother, "for there are many of us engaged in this work. If he spoke sincerely he had evidently reached that state of mind which gains for these unhappy ones another chance to progress upwards. But he was mistaken in thinking that all of the miserable ones here are anxious to deter their friends on earth from leading such lives as they themselves lived there.

"That, unhappily, is far, very far from being the desire of most of those here. For most of them have not repented. They are still utterly selfish. They feel no sorrow for those whom they wronged on earth. It is of themselves only they think. It is because of their own misery only that they shed tears.

"The depths of selfishness, wickedness and depravity to which some natures sink on earth you little comprehend. But we, who minister to such as these in the underworld, know, for we can read their thoughts. And when we read therein indications that some of them are attaining to less selfish states of mind and are beginning to repent of their misdeeds and wasted opportunities on earth, we go to them and try to shed light on their darkened understandings, tell them that there is yet hope for them, speak to them of God and His wonderful love, and encourage them to make further spiritual progress, until they reach that state which enables us to take them from this wretched place.

"For it is never the will, nor the desire of the loving Father that any of His children, however far they may stray from Him, and however wicked and degraded they may become, should endure misery and torment throughout all eternity. Always, always, there is a path open to them, long, laborious and painful as the way must needs be for many of them, by which they may return to Him."

The spectacle of evil spirits on earth, tempting human beings to do evil, had perplexed me greatly, and I asked my brother if it were possible that I could obtain an explanation of this.

"All the mysteries of God's ways are yet far from being fully understood by us," he replied, "far less can they be understood by those who still abide on earth. Let it suffice you then to know that for a good and wise purpose which redounds to the glory of God—as does all else that is now, to many on earth, seemingly inconsistent with that infinite love which we know He is—evil spirits, are at times, permitted to return to earth. And there they are allowed to exercise a certain freedom of choice in what they do, whereby they prove whether the seeds of genuine repentance have yet taken roots in their darkened souls."

TWENTY-FOUR

*M*y *angel guests* had not been long with me one night when my brother said: "I must leave you soon; there is work awaiting me. I am going to conduct to another sphere some of those unfortunate spirits whom I have been privileged to rescue in the underworld."

I expressed a desire to accompany him that I might learn something of their upward progress.

"You may be allowed to do so," he said. "Perhaps you will be able to accompany me to-night."

It is almost invariably only after I have fallen asleep that I am able to leave this world in my spirit body and enter other spheres of existence. How long I had been sleeping I do not know, but once more, by a pathway of light I entered the gloomy forest. As on my two previous visits I beheld there thousands of dark-hued spirits weeping and wailing. Guided, it seemed to me, by some invisible influence, I walked through the forest until I reached the canyon in the depths of which flowed the dark stream that I have likened to a river of tears.

On the further side was my brother, and gathered about him were some thirty spirits, presenting, in their dark robes, a striking contrast to his radiant form. My brother came to me, and together we passed over the river and joined the waiting group. Their general appearance was like that of those in the forest on the other side of the stream whose wailings I could still hear, but their faces wore a different expression. Expectancy had taken the place of despair. Hope had dawned for them. They were quiet. No longer, seemingly, were they obsessed by the demon of unrest.

We traversed what appeared to me a long distance, I walking by my brother's side, and the spirits whom he had rescued following us. We had not gone far when the ground began to slope sharply upwards and so continued until we reached the journey's end. On earth such a walk would have fatigued me greatly, but in my spirit body I was not sensible of any fatigue.

As we ascended the slope, which was thickly wooded, the atmosphere, which in the underworld forest was dense, murky

146

and oppressive, gradually grew clearer, the foliage of the trees became more abundant and greener, and the grass more verdant.

At last we reached what appeared to me to be a vast plateau. It was covered with trees. Its general aspect was much like that of a forest on earth in the temperate zone as seen on a dull day when the sky is gray and the sun hidden. There were birds there and they sang sweetly.

In the space over which my sight was able to range there were thousands of spirits. It was obvious from their bearing that the burden of sin lay much less heavily upon them than upon the despair-stricken wretches in the gloomy forest whence we had come. Their robes were not dark, but of a dull gray color, and I noticed that the robes of those who had followed us were now of the same hue.

"It is good to be where one can hear the birds sing," I heard one of these latter exclaim. Others expressed their delight in the green of the grass and the trees. Some gave vent to their feelings in tears, but they were tears of joy.

Many spirits came forward and greeted the newcomers kindly and led them away.

Extending through an avenue in the forest I discerned a long row of small, low structures that might be likened to huts. They were all alike and of a dull gray color.

"They are places of rest for those who live here," my brother explained. "To them they can retire for meditation and communion with the angels who minister to them. In the sphere from whence we came there are no such places, for there there is no rest."

I looked within one of them. The interior consisted of a single small chamber, which was bare and of the same dull gray hue as the exterior.

"How different from the beautiful rest chambers in the Heavenly Garden!" I exclaimed.

"That difference," said my brother, "is indicative of the difference between the spiritual states of those who dwell here and of those who have ascended to the heavenly spheres."

I saw no flowers in this sphere, nor did I hear any glad outbursts of praise and thanksgiving such as delighted me in the Heavenly Garden. The only songs I heard were those of the birds.

"This sphere," said my brother, "is the first of these spheres which lie between the underworld whence we came—which is not the lowest of the underworlds—and the heavenly spheres. The lot of those here is much better than that of those who abide in the gloomy forest. Here they are far more amenable to the instruction and guidance of the angels from the heavenly spheres who minister to them and help them to progress spiritually, for all progress with us is spiritual.

"From time to time, as they become fitted for such labor, they are permitted to go to the underworld which you have seen, and minister to the wretched ones there. Thereby they

148

are helped to rid themselves of selfishness, which is the greatest obstacle to spiritual growth."

I remarked that I was glad he had succeeded in rescuing so many from the underworld.

"I rejoice, too, that I have been able to do such work in God's service," he answered. "But from your world, through the portals of death, a host of sin-stricken souls pass daily to the gloomy underworlds. It is in your world that we are most anxious to see the light—the knowledge—spread, that will deter large numbers from leading the sinful, wicked, selfish, godless lives that bring them to such a state of misery and wretchedness after death. For after death the law, 'As you sow so shall you reap,' must be fulfilled. And it is harder—much harder—to reform and reclaim godless sinners in the gloomy underworlds than it is in the world in which they pass their physical lives.

"Could earth's children be made to realize that life on earth is but the prelude to the never-ending life, that it depends on their earth life whether they sink to depths of wretchedness, misery and despair far more hopeless and acute than can be experienced on earth, or whether they enter a state of existence more joyous far than can be found on earth—could they be made to realize this, it is inconceivable that so many would, as they now do, neglect to prepare themselves for that eternal life.

"Selfishness would then be seen to be suicidal. Christ's

149

precepts and injunctions would then be recognized as the most eminently sound and practical that were ever given to mankind. The world would not then long present the sorry spectacle it now does to the angels, in which the generous bounty of nature, the gift of the Creator to His children on earth, is so largely utilized to minister to the selfish greed of the few instead of to the happiness and well-being of all. And then to the under-worlds there would no longer come such a continuous stream of wretched, sin-laden, poverty-stricken souls.

"Life on earth, rightly understood, provides an admirable training school for the eternal life that follows it. Its struggles against material obstacles, its conflicts with temptations both from within and from without, are the means by which strength of character is developed and spiritual growth attained. These are the possessions that survive death and prove precious treasures here."

TWENTY-FIVE

In attempting to convey to the minds of others, by means of this book, some conception of the beauties, wonders and mysteries of the spirit spheres to which I have been taken, I have felt deeply my unfitness for the task. It would have been much better performed by one of the many gifted and saintly ones of earth, had such an one been granted the same exalted privileges. But to me has been assigned the task of giving some account of what has been revealed to me, and I must continue with it, though what I have now to relate would require an inspired pen to describe at all adequately.

Often in my spirit body I have ascended to the Courts of

Light, as the angels call them. When I have gone to the Heavenly Garden I have always been conscious of being taken there by one of the angels, and nearly always by my guardian angel. But when I have ascended to the Courts of Light I have not been conscious of being taken there. I have suddenly awakened to find myself there with the angel whom I have learned to call the Mentor standing by my side. Before I met him there, this angel, who is indeed one of the wisest and most faithful of spiritual counsellors, had often appeared to me and instructed me. It was he who, as related in a previous chapter, gave me an insight into the meaning of that phrase, "Poverty and riches are of the spirit."

When I first found myself in the Courts of Light I was standing with the Mentor in the center of a large court or square, close to a beautiful white fountain with three basins, one above the other, and surmounted by a nude statue, the idealized embodiment of everything it is possible to conceive of grace and symmetry in the male human figure. The right arm is extended above the head, and in the hand is grasped a wreath—the wreath of victory. From the fountain the spray rises high and falls with a melodious tinkle into the basins.

The light is very bright. To the physical eyes it would be a dazzling brightness, but it does not dazzle the eyes of the spirit body. There is a wondrous quality of exhilaration in the fragrant atmosphere. One is filled there with an exuberant sense of life in which one is utterly unconcious of those

152

limitations which on earth the physical body seems to impose on the indwelling spirit. There the spirit feels that it is indeed free.

On the four sides of the court—the only one of the many courts in the Courts of Light that I have yet seen—are magnificent buildings and temples in the Grecian style of architecture. They reminded me of pictures I had seen and descriptions I had read of the Acropolis of Athens before time and barbaric hands had wrought such havoc there.

For me to attempt to describe their wondrous beauties, so that others might obtain therefrom some adequate idea of them, would be utterly futile. I must leave that to the imagination of those who have some knowledge of Grecian art. If they will summon before their mental visions everything that has aroused them to enthusiasm in what they have seen, or read, of Grecian architecture and sculpture, and then strive to impart to them that indescribable spiritual quality with which every object in the heavenly spheres is invested, they will obtain a far better idea of the Courts of Light and their temples of art than they would derive from any labored attempt of mine to portray them in words, ignorant as I am of art and its phraseology.

Tall, of majestic mien and commanding presence, with a broad, high forehead and finely chiselled features, the Mentor appears to me a glorified embodiment of the noblest type of ancient Greek manhood. His costume is that of classic Greece and his garments are white, but of a whiteness unlike those of any earthly garments, for they radiate light. Around his head is a circlet of leaves, and on his brow, attached to a slender fillet of gold, is a glittering star.

Other angels, similarly attired, were standing or walking about the court, in groups or couples, conversing earnestly.

As I can only suggest the glorious beauties of the Courts of Light, so, I fear, I can only suggest the wondrous charm and impressiveness of the Mentor's discourses, and again must appeal to the imagination of my readers that they may form some conception of them.

Let them imagine themselves listening to one of the wisest men of the halcyon days of Greece. Let their imaginations take a further flight, and conceive of themselves as listening to that same man as he would be had he continued to live on earth for more than two thousand years with his mental faculties and physical vigor unimpaired. And if their imaginations are equal to the further effort, let them conceive of themselves as listening to such an one whose mind through all these ages has been developing and expanding in the angelic spheres where he is now one of the high-raised angels. If they can do this, they will understand why I, still a child of earth and a simple-minded one, whose life has been too full of work to allow leisure for culture, shrink from the thought of daring to attempt to convey to others anything approaching an adequate idea of what fell from his lips when I listened entranced to him in the Courts of Light. And yet the attempt must be made, for these revelations have not been made to me that they may be locked up as a sacred treasure in my own breast.

The difficulty lies not in repeating from memory words and phrases that he used—for he adapted his language to my understanding as a grown man does when he speaks to a little child—but in depicting the wondrous power with which, coming from such an one, they were invested.

Everyone who has listened to public speakers knows what a difference the personality of the speaker makes as regards the extent to which his utterances carry conviction. Yet when listening to the most magnetic and eloquent of speakers here the mind still feels free to question their statements and to debate their conclusions, and perhaps reject them as false. But when listening to the Mentor in the Courts of Light it is impossible to maintain that attitude of mind. I am convinced, then—nay, more, I know absolutely—that I am listening to truths—spiritual truths—of the highest importance to mankind.

When I have returned to earth after listening to him I have sometimes written down carefully what I remembered of what he had said to me. But when I have read over what I have written I have discovered, sadly, that the words no longer possess that power which brought such glorious conviction to my own heart when I heard the Mentor utter them. Then I am in despair and wish that I possessed that gift which great writers have, and by means of which I could make others feel what the Mentor made me feel.

For the Mentor, who lived several hundred years before Christ began His ministry on earth, is a servant of the Master in the Courts of Light. And the great truths which he burned into my heart were the truths which the Savior proclaimed in Galilee. The burden of his discourse was ever God's love and the blessedness and happiness it confers on those who accept it.

"The souls of many," he said to me, "are calling for more light—light to guide them to God, the great All-Father. And there before them, if they would only see it, shines the light they need, the only light by which their souls can find peace, the light of God's love as revealed to them in Christ, the loving Savior, who has spoken to them in such tender accents, 'Come unto me, and I will refresh you,' 'Come unto Me, and I will give you rest.'

"To all who earnestly seek to know God and to open their hearts to Him, He sends His holy angels to minister to them, to give them spiritual guidance and comfort that they may realize they are truly God's children and precious in His sight.

"There are angels, hosts of angels, eager, anxious, longing, yearning to minister to mankind, to persuade them to open the windows of their souls to the light—God's light—which brings with it that peace of mind that passeth all understanding.

"But because most of them dwell in spiritual darkness and

156

worship false gods—the gods of selfish gain, of earthly fame or sensual pleasures—or are so depressed by poverty and misery that they do not even realize they have souls, the angels cannot minister to them as they so fervently wish to do.

"Few among the many millions of mankind know anything of the angels or their ministry on earth. Most of their spiritual teachers are equally ignorant. They believe that the angels remain always in heaven, enjoying bliss unspeakable themselves, but heedless, forgetful of struggling, suffering mankind on earth whose souls are starving.

"As we rise higher in the heavenly spheres we gain a deeper, broader knowledge of God's love. To the extent that we realize it do we, ourselves, reflect, though feebly it seems to us, God's attributes. And as God's love for His children on earth is no less than His love for His children in the heavenly spheres, how could we be what we are and not love them also?

"Even as your heart, sister, is moved to compassion by seeing one on earth who is starving and you gladly give him of your means that he may obtain food, so are we, to a greater extent, filled with compassionate yearning to feed the starving souls of God's many millions—to bring to them the wonderful gift of God's love."

Then, as though to give fuller expression to the fervor of his feelings, he sang these lines, which I had never heard sung by earthly voices, though perhaps they may be found in some collection of hymns.

157

It speaks to my heart once again,
The sweet and the joyous refrain,
Sing it again and again,
The wonderful gift of God's love,
Sing it again and again,
The wonderful gift of God's love.

The words are simple, but, oh, what a depth of meaning there was in them as the Mentor sang them with such fervid exultation! Such singing is never heard on earth. Never before had I heard anything that so deeply impressed me with the reality of God's love.

Although I have placed them in quotation marks, I do not pretend to have given the exact words as used by the Mentor. Few who have been held spellbound by a brilliant speaker can reproduce from memory, in the order in which they were delivered, the very words, phrases and sentences that have stirred the deepest depths of their natures. But I have faithfully reproduced the substance and spirit of one of the Mentor's talks. Yet I am mournfully conscious how far it will fail to bring to the minds of those who read it what it brought to my mind when I heard it.

I must appeal once more to the imagination of my readers to help me. Let them again picture the wondrous Courts of Light, and the Mentor as the high-raised angel, and let them imagine themselves listening to him, as I listened to him, standing by the beautiful fountain.

158

If they can do this, perchance they, too, may feel what I felt, and the wonderful gift of God's love will sink deep into their souls.

When I returned to earth, I know not how, it was to find myself again in my physical body and lying in bed. But that wondrous burst of song was still ringing in my ears.

TWENTY-SIX

*A*gain *I found myself* with the Mentor, standing by the fountain in the Courts of Light. He filled a crystal goblet with water and handed it to me.

"Drink deep of this," he said, "it will refresh and strengthen you."

I drained the contents of the goblet and felt immediately invigorated, and all my spiritual faculties seemed to be quickened. The Mentor then raised his hands above my head and made a gesture as though throwing something upon me, and I found myself clad in a shimmering white robe.

"Now come with me," he said, "and I will show you one of the temples of art."

He led me some distance through the Court until we reached an imposing building of purest white marble, so it seemed to me. Its style of architecture was that of a Grecian temple. Ascending a broad flight of steps, we passed under a pillared portico and entered a spacious hall. The walls were draped in rich crimson, but the texture of the material, if such it can be called, was cloudlike. When I tried to touch it I could feel nothing.

The interior was filled with statuary—single figures and groups—all, in appearance, of marble. Interspersed among them were palms. The air was filled with a delicious fragrance.

The exquisite beauty of the statuary thrilled me with admiration. Some of the pieces I recognized from reproductions and photographs which I had seen in art galleries. I was particularly attracted by the figure of Hermes, because the head is much like that of the Mentor, except that his chin is squarer, his brow higher, and his general expression indicative of a more resolute will and greater intellectual power. But this statue and all the other statues in the hall were possessed of an indefinable something which differentiated them from any statuary I had seen on earth and rendered them more beautiful. I asked the Mentor what it was.

"What you see here," he replied, "are the embodiments of the ideals of some of the most famous masters of antiquity, which they strove to render visible and tangible. And though their works were rightly acclaimed masterpieces on earth, what

162

they wrought there, as you can see by comparison with those works, still fell short of the ideals they had in their minds, as is always the case with the work of human hands."

"And whence came these beautiful works of art?" I asked.

"They came at the command of the Supreme, as did all else that you see here," he answered. "It is only the works of the Creator that are perfect.

"For many generations," he went on, "there has been no improvement in the sculptor's art on earth. The works of the masters of ancient Greece have never been surpassed. When I dwelt on earth the acquisition of such works was my chiefest pleasure. I delighted in their beauty. But long since I learned that the pleasure derived from such a source is far inferior to the joy experienced by those who seek to grow in the spiritual life, to acquire an abiding faith and trust in God, and to help others to develop spiritually."

I told him that I had ardently wished often that I had been endowed with talents that would have enabled me to portray on canvas, or to mold in clay, some of the beautiful visions that had at times haunted my imagination.

"A far greater gift has been bestowed on you," he said. "Yours is the exalted privilege to visit these heavenly spheres, and to tell others something of what has been revealed to you of God's infinite love and of the ministry of His angels, and to sow the seeds that will bear good fruit in many hearts. A great work of art may gain the admiration of thousands, and

163

obtain some measure of earthly fame for the artist, but far better it is to win even one soul for God. There are many who have been acclaimed great on earth whose rewards after death have been obtained not by those things for which they were remembered on earth, but by deeds of which those who applauded them so loudly knew nothing, and which would have added nothing to their fame had they been known."

We left the temple and walked a short distance in the Court. The Mentor suddenly stopped, and, making a sweeping gesture, exclaimed, "Behold!"

The beautiful buildings vanished from my sight and I beheld a vast, shining host of angels, singing songs of praise and thanksgiving, in which I was irresistibly impelled to join. It was a sublime and glorious spectacle, for here indeed was joy and happiness manifested such as one can only dimly conceive on earth.

"Oh!" I cried, "if only people on earth could obtain just one glimpse of this! With such a goal to strive after they would never feel that life is not worth living."

It seemed to me that there was an endless procession of the shining throng. I exclaimed at their number.

"The angels of God are as the sands on the seashore," said the Mentor. "They are innumerable. And to you it has been given to tell the children of earth that which will lead many of them to open their hearts to the blessed ministry of these angels. Rejoice and be glad!"

164

I had been several times to the Courts of Light before I was taken beyond the confines of the Court which I saw when I first found myself there. As on previous visits, the Mentor had given me a goblet of water from the fountain to drink, and had caused me to be arrayed in a shining white robe. Then he said, "Come with me and I will show you something of this place that you have not yet seen."

He led me through the Court until we came to a lofty gateway with a beautifully carved gate which resembled bronze. He raised his hand and it swung open. Then I beheld a scene whose entrancing beauty I can only suggest. To use a term which, to my mind, will best serve to indicate its character and charm I would liken it to a vast park, but a park lovelier far than the most famous of English parks. Many of the trees were covered with blossoms, as are our English horse-chestnut trees in early summer. The blossoms were of various sizes and colors, but all of the most exquisite beauty and exhaling a delicious fragrance. Birds were numerous. All that I observed were of brilliant plumage, and they sang as though their very beings were filled to overflowing with exuberant joy. The ground was undulating, and in the distance were silvery streams and lakes and mountains gemmed with sparkling cascades and waterfalls. I stood spellbound by the glorious beauty of the scene. The Mentor asked me what I most admired on earth.

"The beauties of nature," I told him. "The birds, the trees,

165

the flowers have given me greater happiness there than, save rarely, I could derive from human companionship. Often they seem to speak to me, but I am never able to express in words what they say to my soul."

"Then, Joy," he said, "you shall take back with you some of these blooms."

I tried to break some from their stems but discovered, to my surprise, I could not detach a single bloom. The Mentor plucked some for me with, seemingly, the greatest ease.

When I returned in my spirit body to my home I placed them in a vase, but when, next morning, in my physical form, I went to look at them, I discovered that though I could see them as plainly as when the Mentor had handed them to me, and could still smell their exquisite fragrance, they were not palpable to my touch. I could not handle them. My hands passed through them, as they would through a ray of light, and still they remained unbroken with not a single petal deranged.

Save myself, no member of my household could see them or smell them. The angels who visit me in my home can handle them, just as we do earthly flowers. But the latter, of which I always have some in my home, they cannot handle. They see them as I see them, but they offer no resistance to their touch. Their spirit hands pass through them as do my human hands through the heavenly flowers. Therein lies a mystery of which I am unable to give any explanation. Which is the world of solid realities, and which of intangible appearances? Our world or the spirit worlds?

166

But of this I am certain. Wherever the heavenly spheres may be, were it possible for a human being, in human form, possessed only of the five senses which science recognizes, to be transported to them, he could see nothing of their wondrous beauties; could hear not a note of their glad music. To him they would be but empty and silent space. But to me, because it is in my spirit body and endowed with the spirit senses that I am transported to these spheres, they appear more real, more enduring and lovelier far than any portion of this seeming solid earth.

TWENTY-SEVEN

*S*everal *times* the Mentor has taken me to a beautiful temple in the Celestial Park, as I will call it. It is in the Grecian style of architecture, as are all the buildings that I have seen in the Courts of Light. It contains no statuary, nor anything that would correspond to a rostrum or pupit. But each time I have been there, there were many angels seated within, all gazing in the same direction and with a rapt expression on their upturned faces, as though they were listening to some one who was telling them that which it rejoiced their souls to hear.

The Mentor told me that the temple was devoted to meditation—to meditation on the Infinite God and His wonderful love, mercy, goodness and power. And as when earth's children, with minds from which all selfish and discordant thoughts are banished, yield themselves to the deepest yearnings of their souls, they receive holy and uplifting thoughts, so do the angels gathered in the Temple of Meditation, in a far more bounteous measure, because their spiritual capacities are greater and their hearts purer, receive from the Most High that which enriches their souls.

On one of my visits to this temple, without the application of any mechanical contrivance that I could discern, one whole side, composed of what looked like solid marble, was raised, as a curtain might be raised disappearing in the roof, and disclosing a vista of transcendent beauty. At such times there was always seen a procession of white-robed angels, singing glad songs of praise. And oh, how gloriously they sang! They seemed to me to give audible expression to that holy joy with which those in the temple were filled.

There always joined us in the temple an angel who must have finished his life on earth at a great age, for the snows of many winters are on his head, and he has a long, flowing white beard. His aspect is most venerable and indicative of great wisdom and holiness. But, as I have previously noted, the appearance of advanced age in angels is never linked with feebleness or infirmity as with human beings. A buoyant, joyous vigor, far exceeding, so it impressed me, that of the best trained athletes here, is possessed by all the angels in the heavenly spheres, whether they look, as we judge looks here, young or old. And thus, combined as it were with eternal youth, old age—or seeming old age I should perhaps say—is invested with a wondrous charm.

The Venerable, as I will designate him, always left the temple with us and walked with us in the park. I will not attempt to describe the charm of his personality. There is something in his very presence—a something that seems to radiate from him as it does from the Mentor—which lifts one above the trivialities of life.

"It is well," he said to me on one of these walks, "that those here and those on your plane of existence should meditate often and deeply on the love and mercy and greatness of God the All-Father. In this way spiritual knowledge is acquired— not as knowledge of material things is obtained through laborious study by the limited mental faculties, but by simply absorbing the thoughts that flow into the soul."

I made some comment on the expression of joyous absorption which I had observed in the faces of those in the temple.

"What you saw," said the Venerable, "is to be seen only on the faces of those who have attained to that which God demands of His children."

"And what is that?" I asked.

"Truth," he answered—"truth in thought; in that mind which is hidden from men but whose workings are known to God; singleness of purpose, and that purpose devotion to the service of God—to the highest good in what measure soever it is revealed to each individual.

"In your world this is rare. Under the guise of serving God —of doing God's will—men often seek to gain their own ends. With one hand, as it were, they would keep a close grip on God, while with the other they cling to the worthless things of earth. Their minds are divided. Truth cannot abide in them. They may deceive others; they may deceive themselves—and self-deception is fatal to spiritual growth—but God they cannot deceive.

"Seek, then," he went on, "to build on absolute devotion to truth in thought, word and deed. Then your soul rises above those things which would drag it down, obscure its vision, and shut out from it the light of Divine love. Then is given to you, as to every one who thus seeks to learn of God, instruction in spiritual things. Cultivate the habits of listening to that still, small voice which then speaks to your soul, and yield unquestioning obedience to the guidance which is then given you, for at such times truth is revealed to you to the full measure of your capacity to receive it."

On another occasion after we had left the Temple of Meditation the Venerable said: "You have seen what you may attain to, but in reaching out after the ideal beware of overlooking and neglecting the duties of life—of your life on earth. If you do so, you do not learn aright the most useful lessons of life. Life is not given on earth to be dreamed away. It is by

172

the faithful performance, day by day, of its duties, of its tasks, be they great or small, in whatever field one is called on to labor, that the soul acquires patience, strength and steadfastness. To aspiring souls much that lies in the path of duty is often very irksome, especially for those whose lot in life is a narrow one and who must needs earn a livelihood for themselves and those dependant on them by work that is uncongenial. But, believe me, it is by devotion to duty they best prove their faith and trust in the great All-Father and draw near to the great heart of Divine Love."

"It is true," the Mentor added. "Difficulties overcome, trials bravely borne, are the true stepping-stones to the ideal life which ever beckons all aspiring souls. Then live each day as though it were your last on earth. Fulfill its tasks to the best of your ability as unto God. And then retire to rest with a prayer of thanksgiving to your Heavenly Father, feeling assured that whether you awake in heaven, with all life's cares left behind, or awake to another day on life's battlefield, you are in God's hands and all is well."

On one of these walks with the Mentor and the Venerable, I remarked, as I had done in the Heavenly Garden, "You have no sea here."

The Venerable smiled and raised his hand.

"Behold!" he said.

Before he spoke we had been walking amid the beautiful flowering trees and in the distance towered the mountains.

173

When he uttered that one word, "Behold!" the mountains vanished from my sight, and it seemed to me that we were standing on the edge of a cliff and far below us was a vast, glittering expanse of sea on which were many steamers and sailing vessels. It was a sublime spectacle.

"The earth, the sea, the sky, mankind, the universe, all proclaim the omnipotence of the Creator, the great All-Father," said the Mentor. "Drink your fill of the wonders and beauties of His creation, and feel that you, too, have a place in the Divine plan."

Although we were, it appeared to me, a great height above the sea, it was not as one would see such a scene on earth when looking down upon it from a great height that I beheld it. My vision was telescopic—more than telescopic—for the optical laws which pertain to the angle of vision no longer existed for me. I had but to fix my gaze on any one craft, and I could see it and all upon it—the faces of the crew, the shining brass railings, the coils of rope and the various paraphernalia on the deck—as plainly as though I stood upon the deck myself. Nay more, I could see through the decks of a great ocean liner and behold its vitals, see the wondrous machinery and the stokers, bare to the waist, feeding the insatiate furnaces.

The Mentor has told me that the angels have but to fix their thoughts on any spot on earth and instantly they can see it as though they were actually there. They can hear what is said

174

by the people who may be there. They can read the thoughts which are in their minds, which are very different at times from the words to which they give utterance. And from their exalted spheres they can flash, as it were, thought messages to the children of earth which, if their minds be rightly attuned, will find lodgment in them, as the receiving instrument, pitched to the right key, records the wireless electrical message.

Apart from its entrancing beauty, what most impressed me in the Celestial Park, as it did also in the Heavenly Garden, was the entire absence of anything indicative of decay. No fallen leaves, no faded blossoms, no withered blades of grass were to be seen. Even in the vegetation of these blissful realms it would seem that death is unknown.

Nor are there any shadows there. The trees, the buildings, the angels cast no shadows. Whatever is the source of light there it would seem that it does not come from any one central orb, like the sun which illumines the earth. Darkness there is unknown. And on earth, the angels have told me, darkness does not exist for them. They can see here just as well by night as by day. The spirit sight needs no artificial illuminant.

Of the extent of the spheres which I have been privileged to visit in my spirit body I have no knowledge. I can claim to have seen no more of them than might an inhabitant of some other planet see of this world of ours who should chance to alight on it anywhere.

175

TWENTY-EIGHT

O*ften the Mentor* has given me instruction in spiritual matters. I wish that I could impart it to others as it was imparted to me. But though I feel deeply my inability to do justice to his teachings I will endeavor to give the substance of another of his discourses.

"The great secret of peace of mind, of joyous and more abundant life, is trust in God. That is the great lesson taught by the Bible. Rightly understood, in that passage in the Book of Proverbs, 'Whoso hearkeneth unto Me shall dwell safely and shall be quiet from fear of evil,' there is more that will help man to live on earth as he should live than he can obtain from all the systems of philosophy that have ever been written.

"That counsel of the Psalmist, 'In all thy ways acknowledge Him, and He will direct thy paths,' devoutly followed, will be productive of greater happiness by far than can be gained from the most lavish devotion to the guidance of any human teacher whose wisdom is the product of his own understanding alone.

"It is God's love, and that alone, that will satisfy the needs of the soul. To awaken man to that knowledge, to reveal to him what that love is and what it does for him is the mission of the angels on earth. Not from them, however high-raised, can he obtain that which will satisfy the deepest cravings of his nature. That peace of God which passeth all understanding God alone can bestow. And it is through perfect trust in Him and acceptance of His infinite love that it is obtained. As one of your modern poets has written:

> 'Tis heaven alone that is given away,
> 'Tis only God may be had for the asking.

"The mind of man can find in the world about him, as he beholds it and takes cognizance of it with his material senses, no satisfactory evidence of the existence of an omnipotent Creator, still less will he be able to discern proof that the Creator is a being of infinite love. Laws of nature, as he terms them, he will discover seemingly cruel and pitiless often, and from them he may deduce the existence of a supreme law-giver who sets in motion forces, physical and moral, of irresistible power and lets them work, indifferent utterly as to whom they

178

bless and whom they destroy. But he will discover no proof that will satisfy his reason that from God he can obtain comfort when in trouble; courage when sorely beset; strength when his own strength fails him; hope when he is in despair.

"It is only by spiritual understanding that this knowledge can be acquired. The spiritual understanding apprehends spiritual truths by their effect—by the glow of delight which they kindle in the soul. It is only the spiritual understanding which can apprehend the love of God.

"The love of God is not a mere abstraction; it is something real; it is the most potent force in the world. It is to the soul of man what the sun is to the earth on which he dwells. Deprived of the life-giving heat and light of that sun the earth will yield man nothing that will satisfy his physical hunger. He may dig and plow and sow, but nothing will ripen for him.

"And the soul that is shut off from the fructifying light of divine love will yield nothing that will satisfy the needs of the spiritual nature for sustenance. The man who ignores God, whose soul is never illumined by the glorious light of divine love, despite the most laborious efforts of his own intellect, however gifted he may be, can find no satisfactory answer to the deep problems of existence which press upon every earnest nature for solution. But as the magnetic needle turns to the pole so does the soul, under the influence of divine love, turn to the Heavenly Father and hearken unto Him. Then do the doubts and perplexities that assailed him when he

179

trusted solely to the guidance of his own reason vanish. Peace wraps him round. His fears are dispelled. He feels that wisdom far higher than his own is counselling him, and that which he has yearned to know, that which alone will give him peace of mind, is being revealed to him. He realizes then that God does indeed exist, and that God is directing his paths.

"To attain that state of mind which renders him accessible to the ministry of angels and brings his soul into communion with his Maker, man must cease his own mental struggles. He must acknowledge his own inability to find that which his soul needs. He must yield himself to that instinct of prayer which is implanted in all hearts. He must pray for help. Be it in words or in a voiceless longing, it matters not so that it be sincere. Prayer is the great purger of the soul of those things which keep it from hearkening unto God. By prayer he enters the silence where all jarring discords are stilled. And there, reverently and humbly, he should await the answer to his prayer.

"It should not be expected in material and tangible form. Nor in audible words. But in the thoughts and feelings that are impressed upon him. For it is at such times there is revealed to man the truth that makes him free—free from fear in all its varied forms—and he partakes of that blessedness which is found in rest in the Lord."

"Fear," said the Mentor at another time, "is the greatest

180

enemy of mankind. Countless millions pass the greater part of their lives in bondage to some forms of it—fear of sickness, fear of failure, fear of poverty, fear of old age, fear of death. The man only half lives whose mind is a constant prey to dark forebodings of trouble. Fear paralyzes the mental faculties and makes of the imagination, which should be a source of constant delight, an instrument of torture. It is only by trust in God that man can be delivered from this terrible scourge.

"And yet there are many people who hold aloof from everything that would awaken their spiritual understandings, from a mistaken belief that to yield to their promptings would involve a narrowing of the range of their mental activities; that it would restrict them to a life that they regard as somber and depressing; that, in short, the spiritual life necessitates a great sacrifice of happiness.

"How soon they would learn the contrary could they be got to open their hearts to the ministry of angels! Did not the Master say, 'Take My yoke upon you, for My yoke is easy and My burden is light'? It is only the man who has learnt the great spiritual truths of life whose mind is really free. Thereby all his mental faculties are quickened. The world wears a new beauty for him. His life becomes joyous. Then his imagination can indeed soar—soar to the very heavens."

TWENTY-NINE

In the preceding chapters much has been told of what I have learned of the angels and their ministry, both on earth and in the spirit spheres. I could not have acquired this knowledge had I not been endowed with great psychic powers. The vast majority of people do not possess them.

If the capacity to receive the ministry of the angels, and to realize that help and guidance are being obtained from them, were dependent on the possession of such powers, then most people could not obtain their help, and what a blessed help it may become can be understood only by personal experience.

But, happily, such help is not necessarily restricted to those who have extraordinary psychic faculties.

A friend of mine who disclaims the possession of any unusual psychic powers has obtained the most convincing proof of the ministry of angels, and thereby has been enabled to triumph over a sorrow that otherwise would have crushed him. Because it may help others similarly situated to obtain the same solace and comfort, I have obtained his permission to insert in this book the following account of his experience which he has written for me.

"After a long illness and much suffering, endured with great patience, my dearly loved wife had died, and I was left alone. She had been able, often, to see spirits and to talk to them, and had been wonderfully helped by them. As she had told me what they revealed to her, I, too, had obtained the perfect assurance that death is but the beginning of another state of existence which, for those who strive to lead good lives, is far happier than that on the physical plane. But I had never been able to see spirits myself, or to converse with them as she had done.

"When my dear wife was taken from me, as I had not her psychic powers it was vain to hope, it seemed to me, that I might be able to see her and talk with her, as she had, when alive, seen and talked with her mother and other loved members of her family who had preceded her into the better world. But I longed ardently that I might, in some way, be able to

184

realize her presence and that I, too, might receive help from the spirits in some form.

"It was borne in upon me that by giving way to grief and dejection I raised a barrier between myself and the spirits which would shut me off from their influence. I felt, therefore, that as the first step towards obtaining what I so much desired I should have to rid myself of sad and gloomy thoughts. Instead of dwelling on my own great loss and forlorn condition I made myself think of what she had gained. I pictured to myself, as well as I could, the glorious change that had taken place in her condition. I was then able to realize that all I had often prayed she might obtain had been granted her. Her health had been restored, her strength had been renewed, and she was free from all pain. And far more than I had prayed for had been bestowed upon her, for she had been admitted to heaven.

"'Would you, if you could,' I asked myself, 'summon her back from heaven to dwell again in an enfeebled, pain-racked body, that you might be happier?'

"'No, emphatically, no,' I replied to my own query.

"Then, it seemed to me, I received a message from on high which bade me fall on my knees and thank God that my prayers had been so abundantly answered, and rejoice in the proof that had been vouchsafed me of His goodness and mercy.

"Then peace came to me and my soul found rest. And then, oh, the wonder of it! I realized that she was with me and speaking to me—speaking to my soul. It was not a mere feeling; it was absolute certainty. Impressed thus upon my soul the purport of her thoughts was more clearly apprehended by me, and sank deeper than had they been imparted to me in audible words and reached me through the medium of my own physical ears. In this way my wife, now an angel, was able to make me share in the great joy that had come to her.

"This experience was often repeated. But to obtain the blessed and absolute assurance of her presence and receive her thoughts, I found it necessary always that I should first attain that state of mind which impels one to offer a prayer of thanksgiving to God. This was not always easy. Indulgence in self-pity, resentment for real or fancied wrongs, vain regrets or any similar weakness, would prevent it. Therefore I failed often.

"I formed the habit of devoting an hour or more to this communion before retiring at night. I prepared myself for it —or tried to—by recalling how many proofs of God's loving kindness I had received in the course of the day. Then, if I had been successful in ridding myself of selfish and discordant thoughts, followed the prayer of thanksgiving and the sweet communion with the loved one.

"With practice, my susceptibility to her uplifting influence was much increased. After a little while I was able to realize that other spirits whom I had known and loved here before death had claimed them, were also with me. I was able to

186

identify often, and very clearly, the one from whom came the thoughts that were imparted to me. I found that it helped me greatly to discriminate between my own thoughts and those they gave me to interpret the latter in audible words or to write them out.

"I had not been long availing myself of this blessed solace when I was made aware that there had come to minister to me the spirit of one whom I had not known on earth. This spirit impressed me as one who was possessed of greater power than the other spirits who came to me. The thoughts which I received from him were imparted with greater force and directness. They were always the loftiest that I was capable of receiving and comprehending. Their purpose was to broaden my knowledge of God, strengthen my trust in Him, and give me a better understanding of His love than I had, up to that time, acquired.

"I believe that the power of the spirits to impart spiritual truths is much greater than is possessed by the most gifted of human spiritual teachers. Those whom I had heard preach, and among them were some famous divines, had never given me such help as enabled me to comprehend, at all adequately, the love of God. But through the help of the spirits, and especially the one whom I last mentioned, I have been able to realize, to some extent, what that love is. I have learned that just as one who is in a room in which the atmosphere is dense and stifling can obtain relief by opening wide the windows and

187

filling his lungs with the fresh air of heaven, so can one who realizes what God's love is, obtain spiritual refreshment by opening wide, as it were, the windows of his soul and letting that love in."

God loves all His children and the ministry of His angels is for all mankind.

THIRTY

*O*nce *the Mentor* took me from the Courts of Light, through what seemed to me a vast distance in space, to the summit of a high mountain which was surrounded by lower peaks, all covered with snow.

"Behold!" he said, with a majestic gesture, "the wondrous beauty of the dawn."

The dawn was just beginning to break. The glory of the scene only an inspired pen could portray. On the mountains the color changed from gray to the faintest pink, and from that to a rich, rosy red. In the eastern sky the shifting panorama of color was even more beautiful. It was as though, with an unseen brush, some invisible titanic master artist was painting it with the opalescent tints of the rainbow. And then uprose the sun in majestic splendor, flooding the earth with light and warmth. To me it seemed that I was witnessing the veritable creation of the world.

"There will yet break," said the Mentor, "a more glorious dawn for all mankind," and again he exclaimed, "Behold!"

Looking down I beheld, far beneath me, a vision of earth's toiling millions of all nations and races, in cities, fields and plains.

"All these," said the Mentor, "are toiling for bread, but there is a deeper hunger in their souls which only the Infinite God can satisfy. And as you have seen the rising sun dispel the darkness of night from the earth, so, in the spiritual dawn which is to break for them, will the dark shadows of ignorance, doubt and fear be swept from their minds by the ministry of God's angels, and the knowledge of the love of God will illumine their souls."